INTRODUCTION AND PRACTICAL GUIDE TO
MUSIC EDUCATION

First Edition

By LAURA M. DORNBERGER
and KATHERINE M. LEVY

cognella® | ACADEMIC PUBLISHING

Bassim Hamadeh, CEO and Publisher

John Remington, Senior Field Acquisitions Editor

Kaela Martin, Project Editor

Miguel Macias, Senior Graphic Designer

Trey Soto, Licensing Coordinator

Bryan Mok, Interior Designer

Natalie Piccotti, Senior Marketing Manager

Kassie Graves, Vice President of Editorial

Jamie Giganti, Director of Academic Publishing

Cover images: Copyright © 2016 by iStockphoto LP/FooTToo.

Copyright © 2016 by iStockphoto LP/Instants.

Copyright © 2014 by iStockphoto LP/piola666.

Copyright © 2016 by iStockphoto LP/deepblue4you.

Printed in the United States of America

ISBN: 978-1-5165-3108-0 (pbk) / 978-1-5165-3109-7 (br)

TABLE OF CONTENTS

We offer special thanks to Thomas F. Dornberger for drawing the cartoons for this book. —**Laura Dornberger and Katherine Levy**

INTRODUCTION

The ground beneath your feet...

"A journey of a thousand miles begins with a single step." This is actually an inaccurate translation—often incorrectly attributed to a variety of people and cultures. In fact, Lao Tzu's quote is more accurately translated as "a journey of a thousand *li* starts from where one stands" ("Beginning," 2016). This is to say that a long journey begins with the stillness of where you are—the moments leading up to the first step.

So, where are you? What is beneath your feet? Why choose music education? What about the field is so interesting to you that you want to do it for the rest of your career? What will you bring to the field of music education? The ground beneath you is unique to you, which means that your contributions to your students and to the field of music education will be unique. Finding your path and finding your destination, therefore, begins with finding out who you are and what you want out of this field. Growing from a student into a professional is a crucial journey and one that begins before you ever enter college. Considering these questions and answering them to the best of your ability is the very beginning of your growth … the ground beneath your feet. Only then are you ready for the first step.

So … you want to be a music teacher? Smart choice. Music teaching is challenging, fun, creative, and motivating, and it changes many lives. In just a few short years, you will be in charge of the health, safety, musical growth, and education of hundreds, if not thousands, of children. (Insert panic-induced cold sweat here.)

Granted, the journey to becoming a music educator is not easy, but it is designed to prepare you for each skill and trait you need to become a successful and impactful teacher.

This book is designed to give you an overview of the journey ahead, along with plenty of tips to stay on course, necessary side trips, and potential hazards along the way. Throughout your music education preparation, you will delve into all these topics and more in much greater detail. This overview is designed to help you to begin thinking differently about teaching and to change your lens from a student to a teacher.

As I repeatedly tell my students, it is not about starting great … it is about ending *better*.

Reference

Beginning. (2016). *Oxford essential quotations* (4th ed.). Retrieved July 10, 2017, from http://www.oxfordreference.com/view/10.1093/acref/9780191826719.001.0001/q-oro-ed4-00000846?rskey=Xc3Y Ve&result=291

Image Credit

CHAPTER 1

WHY TEACH MUSIC?

> **Things to consider while reading this chapter:**
>
> 1. Why do you want to be a music teacher?
>
> 2. What do you want your future students to learn from you?
>
> 3. What areas of being a music teacher do you need to improve upon?

Why teach? Why teach music? What is the value of education? These questions have been debated and argued for centuries. Let's take them one at a time.

WHAT IS YOUR REASON FOR WANTING TO TEACH?

Why teach? Why do you want to be a teacher? Why does anyone? Is there a right answer? Maybe, more important, is there a wrong answer? Here are the top five most popular reasons for going into education from my students over the years:

1. "I want to be a music teacher because my music teacher changed my life, and I want to do that for someone else."

2. "I want to be a music teacher because I love music and I love children, so it's a natural choice."

3. "I want to be a music teacher because I love music and performing, but my parents told me I can't make a living as a performer, so I'd better have an education degree as a backup plan."

4. "I want to be a music teacher because I love music and teaching, and it is a great career—summers off, good pay, good benefits, and a stable job."

5. "I want to be a music teacher because my parent/relative/friend/sibling is one, and I have never considered another career."

Is your main reason listed here? Let's look more closely at each rationale and consider its strengths and potential pitfalls.

Reason 1: You want to be a music teacher because your music teacher changed your life, and you want to be that influence to others.

Strengths

That is a noble gesture and probably the most popular answer from my students. You were influenced in a positive manner—so much so that you are pursuing a career in music education so that you can do the same for others. You want to "pay it forward" and pass on this positive experience to others. You want to change lives for the better. You want to make a difference.

Potential Pitfalls

The "mini me" syndrome. When I see a former student who got into teaching for this reason, the conversation often goes something like this:

> **Me:** "Hi! How are you? How is teaching?"
>
> **Former student:** "Great! I have two seniors this year who are going into music in college!"

From this person's answer, we can conclude that the measure of success is how many students followed the same path my former student did—music performance or education. Here is where I tell my students what I am about to tell you:

> Dear Reader,
>
> You are weird. You know you are. I am, too. According to the U.S. Department of Education, National Center for Education Statistics (2016), approximately 3.5 million full-time teachers were working in U.S. public and private schools in 2014. That was approximately 1% of the population of the United States. Now consider that only about 5% of those school teachers are certified music teachers, and you discover that music teachers make up less than 0.0001% of the country's population (about 1 out of every 2,000 people). This is an important statistic to keep in mind. When you are planning how to teach something, and you remember what worked for you when you were learning, remember that you are *not* in the majority. Less than half of 1% of the population got interested in making music and decided to pursue music education as a career, the way you did. That means that more than 99% of your future students will *not* go on to become music teachers. If your goal as a music educator is to teach lots of future "yous," you will have around a 99% failure rate! Therefore, choosing to become a music teacher so that your students will become music teachers or performers is a pursuit that is likely to fail.

Things to Consider

Let's get back to the original answer ... you want to change lives. What does that look like to you? Changing lives does not necessarily mean that your future students will pursue music. You want to alter a person's life in a positive way. What can students do as a result of having you as a teacher? Is it something they wouldn't have gotten, or gotten as well, without having you as a teacher? If a student stayed in school just to go to your class, would that meet your goal of changing lives? Would you be more proud of a graduate of yours who went on to be a principal violinist at a symphony than a student who grew up to work in a factory? How would you know if you had an influence on the second student?

As teachers, we often do not know the impact we have on our students. We hear from a few who have the insight and maturity or kindness to let us know we helped them, but most of the time, we do not. So, what should we look for when deciding whether we are successes or not? Narrow your answer to consider exactly what kind of a difference you want to make in the lives of your students.

Reason 2: You want to be a music teacher because you love music and you love children, so it's a natural fit.

Strengths

Certainly if you love music and love working with children, you may spend the rest of your life very happy in your chosen profession. It is obviously important to like children and music, and when you are excited about a subject and like the people with whom you are working, you have a positive impact on your students' ability to learn.

Potential Pitfalls

Your reason assumes that music education is a profession that is the sum of adding music and children. However, music education is far more complex than that. You may love children, but do you love *teaching* them? Do you love when they make the same mistake over and over and over and over and over again? Do you love when they are making armpit farts during rehearsals? Do you love when they hate the music you love and chose for them to play? The dream for many is to walk into a classroom and pour information and inspiration into young, empty, and impressionable minds. That simply isn't the way young minds work—they are not empty vessels (we'll get to that in a later chapter).

Things to Consider

I tell my students that when a teacher walks into a room full of students, the teacher really becomes the *least* important person in the room. What do your students need? What do they require of you? Teaching is a great career, and, yes, it is often fun. Making the transition from student to teacher is a long process, and part of it is the realization that while children are, of course, cute, they are also thinking, feeling, complex individuals who need our full attention and preparation. Walking into a room of more than 100 instrumentalists or vocalists and teaching them something—not just doing crowd control or behavior management, but *teaching* them something—is fundamentally different from enjoying children and music.

Reason 3: You want to be a music teacher because you love music and performing, but your parents said that you can't make a living as a performer, so they insisted that you have an education degree as a backup plan.

Strengths

(Sounds of crickets in the distance ...)

Potential Pitfalls

Do you want your life to be a backup plan? Really?

Things to Consider

It's one thing to say that you'd love to be a performer or a teacher, so you are going to get an education degree and try to pursue both. It's quite another to say you don't want to be a teacher, but it's a good career choice, so you are going to do it anyway. The best advice I can give you is this: Life is too short to spend it doing something you don't like. It's a hard enough profession when you love it—it's nearly impossible when you don't.

Reason 4: You want to be a music teacher because you love music and teaching is a great career—summers off, good pay, good benefits, and a stable job.

Strengths

This is more of the practical side of career planning. Teaching is a good career, and you are mildly (or more) interested in it, so it seems to be a good choice. Being practical and making choices based on ultimate goals (like planning for a good retirement and having summers off) are smart decisions, especially financially. Yes, teachers do have most summers off (with the addition of in-service days, planning sessions, and professional development days) and good benefits. The job can be stable, after earning tenure, and you can count on having holidays off as well. It is a valid reason to look at a career, not from a romantic view of the difference you will make, but of the practicality behind the job.

Potential Pitfalls

Keep in mind that if this is your main motivation, your priorities may not help you on a day-to-day basis. July and retirement feel very far away in September of any given teaching year. You still need to go in every day and teach and rehearse long hours. If you do not enjoy it or feel fulfilled doing it, a long-term goal like retiring may not be enough motivation to sustain a career.

Things to Consider

Many teachers feel that teaching is a "calling," an inner pull to do something great, but this is certainly not necessary to be a good teacher. It is true that to be an effective teacher, you need to put everything into it and make your students the central focus. If you give the impression that you are a teacher because of July and August, you will have a hard time getting the respect or admiration of your peers. Even though July and August may top many teachers' "favorite things" list, it is essential that your actions demonstrate to your students that you are there for them—that their learning, not your vacation schedule, is your top priority.

Reason 5: You want to be a music teacher because your parent/relative/friend/sibling/etc. is one, and you have never really considered another career.

Strengths

Seeing people you love and respect do something they enjoy is quite a motivation to try it yourself.

Potential Pitfalls

There are many, many, *many* careers out there. Just because you know someone who loves teaching, and it looks like fun, doesn't mean it's the one career for you.

Things to Consider

I encourage you to look into other subjects that might interest you, take a variety of classes outside of music, and research other careers, just to make sure you aren't overlooking something. Then, if you do come to the conclusion that music education is right for you, you can do so with confidence that you picked it because of *you* and not because of someone else.

There is no "correct" reason for becoming a music teacher. The reasons are as varied as the people who decide to pursue it. Having a sense of why you are going to be a teacher, however, is just the first step.

Now that you have more closely considered why you want to be a music teacher, answer these questions:

What are you going to do for your students? What skills, strategies, concepts, and ideas will you teach your students? What is your ultimate goal for your students? Once you answer those questions, you can better focus your attention on gaining the skills necessary to meet those teaching goals.

WHAT MAKES A GOOD MUSIC TEACHER?

We have discussed why you want to be a music teacher; now let's look at what a good music teacher is. First, let's start with what is *good music*? There is music you like and music you don't like, but what's *good*? Remember, when you get your teaching degree and subsequent license, you are a *music* teacher. Not a classical music teacher, but a music teacher. It will be your responsibility to determine what music you have your students study, create, listen to, and perform. You also need to determine what you define as *good* music. For teachers, often what is good music is music that serves a purpose—the purpose of helping your students achieve learning objectives. For example, if you are teaching a I-IV-V progression, jazz music may not be the good music you need, but pop music would be. However, if you are trying to teach improvisation, jazz music could be just the good music you need.

The textbox here contains words that my students consistently use to describe the "perfect" music teacher. Which ones best describe you? How many of these words actually have to do with teachers' musicianship? Just one: "talented." Let's give the benefit of the doubt and say that "knowledgeable" also speaks to musicianship. All the other words listed are personality traits ... *non*-musical personality traits my students have consistently listed as describing the ideal music teacher.

If these words don't describe you perfectly, don't panic. You certainly could still be a successful teacher; however, the descriptors make it clear that the assumption is that teachers must be able to help students in all ways, not just musically. Music teachers are often called upon to be more than teachers of music. Once you are a music teacher, you will be responsible for the general education, musical education, safety, and well-being of hundreds of children in your classes every year. The fact that your school faculty colleagues will join you in those responsibilities means you will have help, but their help will share and define the responsibilities of educating, not reduce them.

Teachers are held to a higher standard of behavior because of the responsibilities they need to shoulder.

INTASC STANDARDS FOR TEACHER CANDIDATES

Below is a list of dispositions, or characteristics, of teacher candidates published by InTASC, the Interstate Teacher Assessment and Support Consortium (Council of Chief State School Officers, 2013). I will discuss each of them next.

Standard 1: Learner Development. The teacher understands how learners grow and develop, recognizing that patterns of learning and development vary individually within and across the cognitive, linguistic, social, emotional, and physical areas, and designs and implements developmentally appropriate and challenging learning experiences.

This standard refers to the ability of teacher candidates to understand child development and the psychological and sociological implications of teaching. It speaks to the need for teachers to understand the learning requirements of the children they teach. An example of this would be choosing music that is age-appropriate in range, content, and teaching approach.

Fig. 1.1: Learners of different ages have different needs.

Council of Chief State School Officers, Selections from InTASC Model Core Teaching Standards: A Resource for State Dialogue, pp. 8–9. Copyright © 2011 by Council of Chief State School Officers. Reprinted with permission

Standard 2: Learning Differences. The teacher uses understanding of individual differences and diverse cultures and communities to ensure inclusive learning environments that enable each learner to meet high standards.

Learning differences occur from student to student and also in larger groups like communities and cultures. Understanding those differences and adjusting your instruction to not only serve but celebrate them is crucial to being an excellent music teacher. Would you plan the same program of music regardless of the needs of the community? Would you include some music that is important to the community? Would you teach your students how to play music that interests them? Are you respectful of others' points of view?

Standard 3: Learning Environments. The teacher works with others to create environments that support individual and collaborative learning, and that encourage positive social interaction, active engagement in learning, and self-motivation.

The key word here is *positive*. Are you a positive influence in the classroom—as a student and as a teacher? Do you ensure that your students are actively participating in their own learning (rather than viewing them as an empty vessel ready to have information "poured" into them), and do you provide your students with the opportunity to play or work with the material so that they can demonstrate their understanding?

Standard 4: Content Knowledge. The teacher understands the central concepts, tools of inquiry, and structures of the discipline(s) he or she teaches and creates learning experiences that make the discipline accessible and meaningful for learners to assure mastery of the content.

For music teachers, this means how well you know your subject area, music, so that you can teach it effectively. Remember that no matter what grade levels you think you would prefer teaching, your license will certify you as a music teacher, Pre-K–12th grade. You need to serve as an excellent role model in music. You need to be able to sing tunefully on pitch. You must be able to play and teach every instrument if you plan to teach instrumental music. If you are pursuing a general music or choral music track, you need to be proficient in piano. Your lack of skill must not stand in the way of your students' learning. You must be able to help your students get better, and in order to do that, you must know what you are doing.

Standard 5: Application of Content. The teacher understands how to connect concepts and use differing perspectives to engage learners in critical thinking, creativity, and collaborative problem solving related to authentic local and global issues.

Fig. 1.2: Understand individual differences and diverse cultures.

This standard requires teacher candidates to be open to a variety of strategies and methods so that they gain the tools they need to enable all of their students to be successful. Being open to different perspectives allows teacher candidates to create classroom environments through which the students are able to learn and succeed in a collaborative and creative manner.

Standard 6: Assessment. The teacher understands and uses multiple methods of assessment to engage learners in their own growth, to monitor learner progress, and to guide the teacher's and learner's decision making.

Fig. 1.3: Did the students understand what you wanted them to learn?

Assessment is crucial for teachers. Simply put, assessment is the way you, as the teacher, know that your students have learned what you set out to teach. Assessment is the feedback you use to inform your instruction. Did the students understand what you wanted them to learn? If so, you move on. Did they seem confused? Then you reteach, teach a different way, revise your thinking to better match what your students understand, and so on.

Standard 7: Planning for Instruction. The teacher plans instruction that supports every student in meeting rigorous learning goals by drawing upon knowledge of content areas, curriculum, cross-disciplinary skills, and pedagogy, as well as knowledge of learners and the community context.

Lesson planning is a critical tool for teachers, especially new teachers. The planning process makes teachers sit down and think through exactly how they will approach a lesson. It allows teachers to notice potential issues and fix them before they teach, and it enables teachers to better instruct because they have a clear plan of not only what the teacher will do, but what the students will do, what they will learn, and how the teacher will know that the students learned the material. Lesson plans also serve as an artifact that maintains a record of what you did in class on a particular day and how you taught it, helping you make plans in future years and revise your lessons and goals from year to year.

Standard 8: Instructional Strategies. The teacher understands and uses a variety of instructional strategies to encourage learners to develop deep understanding of content areas and their connections, and to build skills to apply knowledge in meaningful ways.

Fig. 1.4: Use a variety of instructional strategies.

This standard requires teacher candidates to incorporate a wide variety of strategies to support students' learning—not just learning content knowledge, but also being able to apply that knowledge to other areas. For example, music teachers who make sure their students can sight read a rhythm pattern could deepen students' learning by making sure their students also could recognize that rhythm and perform it correctly in different contexts (hear it in a new key, recognize it in a different piece, compose a piece using that rhythm, etc.).

Standard 9: Professional Learning and Ethical Practice. The teacher engages in ongoing professional learning and uses evidence to continually evaluate his/her practice, particularly the effects of his/her choices and actions on others (learners, families, other professionals, and the community), and adapts practice to meet the needs of each learner.

Good teachers take feedback and apply it in order to get better. They continually seek new ways to teach and develop professionally, and they strive to improve their skills. Can you take constructive criticism and apply it to your future teaching? Do you continue to make the same errors despite being told to fix them? Do you independently seek new experiences and information to improve your teaching? Do you conduct yourself professionally when using social media? Do you behave in such a way as to serve as an excellent role model for children? What changes do you need to make to more easily align yourself with being a professional? All these skills contribute to having a successful disposition for professional learning and ethical practice.

Standard 10: Leadership and Collaboration. The teacher seeks appropriate leadership roles and opportunities to take responsibility for student learning, to collaborate with learners, families, colleagues, other school professionals, and community members to ensure learner growth, and to advance the profession.

Are you an advocate for your students and program? Do you contribute to class discussions? Do you participate to your fullest in each class? Do you ask/answer questions? Are you a leader? If not, you need to become one! Your future students will rely on your advocacy for your program, so you will need to be articulate, purposeful, and persuasive. Raise your hand in your college courses, ask questions, volunteer for student groups, take positions of leadership—learn to be a professional. Learn to communicate with others in a professional manner, even when you are not in a professional setting. Putting something on social media that is seen as insensitive to others can cause you to lose your job. Remember that you are held to a higher standard because you are in charge of children.

Fig. 1.5: Take appropriate leadership roles. Be a professional!

CONCLUSION

Do you see areas of your own strength in the standards above? Do you see areas in which you need improvement? Now is the time to act. Take an honest look at your areas of strength and weakness, and work on those areas that need improvement. Some will naturally improve as you gain knowledge and experience in a teacher preparation program, such as class management, becoming comfortable speaking in front of children, and your overall musicianship. Others areas of your teacher preparation will require your personal initiative and commitment to improve, including secondary instrument knowledge, personal goals for improvement, and content knowledge in your classes.

REFERENCES

Council of Chief State School Officers. (2013, April). *InTASC model core teaching standards and learning progressions for teachers 1.0: A resource for ongoing teacher development.* Washington, DC: Author.

U.S. Department of Education, National Center for Education Statistics. (2016). *Digest of education statistics, 2014* (NCES 2016–006), introduction and chapter 2. Retrieved from https://nces.ed.gov/fastfacts/display.asp?id=28

DISCUSSION QUESTIONS

1. Describe your favorite teacher and your least favorite teacher—what are the similarities/differences between them? What can you learn from them?

2. What are three words you would like your future students to use to describe you? What can you do to make that a reality?

3. Ask your peers and/or family members to write down five adjectives that describe you, and do the same for yourself. Do they match? Do any surprise you?

4. Now that you have seen the dispositions for teachers, what do you see as your greatest challenge in becoming a teacher? How do you plan to use your time throughout college to help overcome that challenge?

5. What do you look forward to most as you look ahead to teaching music?

6. What do you think you can do to help children become more musical?

Credits

CHAPTER 2

A (VERY) BRIEF HISTORY OF MUSIC EDUCATION IN THE UNITED STATES

Questions to think about as you read:

1. What do you think the purpose of music education is today?

2. Think of typical students in each historical era—what challenges did they face when trying to learn music?

Why do music teachers need to know something about the history of public music education? To know where you are going, you need context. For example, if I tell you to go straight for three miles and then turn right, you will get to a variety of destinations unless I first give you a starting point.

MUSIC EDUCATION IN ANCIENT GREECE

Let's start with two main questions: What is the purpose of education? Why teach music? Over the years, these questions have been answered in a variety of ways. The history of your chosen profession really begins in ancient Greece, around 500 BC. The purpose of education for the Greeks was to prepare their citizens to be active participants in society. They taught music because their society included many music festivals and contests, so music needed to be a part of their basic education. Everyone sang and participated in all aspects of a musical life (Mark, 2008). To relate this to today, that means that because people need to be able to sing the National Anthem at a variety of popular venues, students need to learn that song in order to participate in their country's lifestyle. This participation was even more important for the ancient Greeks because there were many aspects of their community life that involved singing and music in general. One needed to be able to sing to be a full participant in society, so people needed to be taught how to sing in schools.

Brain break! *Do you know what amateur means? It does not mean someone who is less talented, less qualified, or less in any other way. It simply means you do something for the love of it. The root words actually mean "to love" and "lover."*

And we're back to ancient Greece. Over the years, the choirs that represented various tribes began to compete with each other as part of public festivities. Once competitions began, everything changed. The increasingly competitive attitude toward singing changed the goal from public participation to winning. Think about it … if your goal is to win, you don't want everyone in your choir—you want *the best* in your choir. If you are not the best, you will find out quickly that your contribution is no longer desired. This competition interest led to more difficult music, and a more elitist view about music making, wherein only the best singers and instrumentalists were encouraged to participate. Elitism is a problem if you are a music teacher. You suddenly do not want or need to educate everyone because everyone isn't going to participate. In elitist society you are only needed to educate those who show promise from an early age. Your job is diminished. Amateurism declined steadily after competition began, and the view that only the talented should perform became the norm (Mark, 2008). This elitist attitude was the first major blow to music education … a fundamental issue still in play today.

MUSIC EDUCATION IN ANCIENT ROME

In ancient Rome, many musicians were slaves. They educated their gifted students in music, and they did so in a scientific, rather than artistic, manner.

The Romans had seven liberal arts:

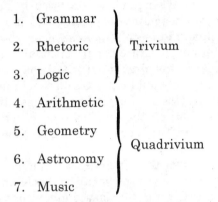

1. Grammar
2. Rhetoric   Trivium
3. Logic

4. Arithmetic
5. Geometry
                Quadrivium
6. Astronomy
7. Music

The first three were called the trivium; only those students prepared to move beyond these three were allowed to study the quadrivium, or the upper four levels of the liberal arts. Instead of studying music as a performance art, these scholars studied music theory as a scientific and mathematical pursuit that could enable one to understand universal truths (Mark, 2008).

EARLY UNITED STATES MUSIC EDUCATION

Moving through time a little more than a thousand years, we arrive at colonial times in the United States, where music education was used to prepare students to be able to participate in church services. (What does that remind you of?) Congregants needed to be able to sing during a church service. At first, this was done in what was called "the old way." This was rote teaching, where the deacon or song leader sang a line and then the congregation sang it back. This meant that congregants did not have to know how to read music, so everyone who could hear the song leader could sing along with the service. However, the quality of congregants' singing soon declined. As with many camp songs today, when something is taught by rote, there is no guarantee that it is consistent from camp to camp or, in this case, church to church. Congregants did not learn many songs, and their accuracy in singing tunes and lyrics was generally poor (Keene, 1982).

In an attempt to improve the quality of participation and understanding of worship services, ministers started to insist that their congregation be taught how to read music. By reading music in hymnbooks, church members could sing songs consistently and accurately. This song leadership of teaching people to read music was called the "new way," teaching "by note" (instead of by rote). Reverend John Tufts took matters of illiterate congregational singing into his own hands and created the first music textbook published in the United States. Through his publications and teachings, Tufts developed a system for using syllables for pitches. He used the already established *fa, sol, la,* and *mi* on the staff instead of what we know as standard notation today. This became known as *fasola* singing (Keene, 1982).

As time went on, more tune books that included rudiments of music became prominent, and church musicians began to teach singing schools. The term *singing schools* refers to classes given, not to buildings. In these singing schools, singing masters taught people (mostly young adults) how to sing by reading simplified notation. Singing schools typically met two evenings per week for two to three months, culminating in a choir performance to showcase learning (Keene, 1982). Singing schools remained a part of American life from the early 1700s to the early 1900s (Mark, 2008).

Singing schools arose from the need for and interest in improving congregational singing. They taught adults and children how to read music and sing, and they often took place in the evening along with classes in other subjects not taught in public schools, such as sewing, dancing, and languages. Some subjects, such as music, were so popular that they eventually became a part of public school education (Mark, 2008). Once the public schools offered music education for free, there was no need to pay for special instruction, which led to the decline of the singing schools.

In 18th- and 19th-century America, society thought of children as small adults who could be part of the workforce and who were not in need of any extra protection. Children often worked on their family's farm and did not attend school at all, or only attended for a few years. If a family could not afford to raise their child, they could sign their child over to a company to be raised in its dorms and to work for the company for sometimes 12 or more hours per day. Companies used children to do dangerous jobs, like mining, because children were able to fit through tiny shafts that adults could not use. Children cleaned dangerous machinery because their hands were small and able to fit into tight spaces. From as early as 1832, there were various groups and coalitions of people who campaigned to regulate or ban child labor, but it was not until 1938 that the U.S. federal government passed the Fair Labor Standards Act, which set limited conditions under which children can be employed, established minimum ages for work, and specified conditions in which children are prohibited from working (Mayer, 2010).

Before children were required to go to publicly funded schools, there were private schools for those who could afford to attend them and schools run by churches. Compulsory education in the United States began in Massachusetts in 1852, when the state required every town to have a primary school that focused on arithmetic and reading. All children were required to attend town school, or their parents would be fined or have their children taken away from them. After this, more states adopted Massachusetts' public school model, until Mississippi became the last state to require education for all children in 1917. Requiring children to be in school not only helped raise the nation's literacy and increase the skills and knowledge of citizens; it also helped reduce occurrences of children being used as cheap labor, because companies now had to send children to school during daytime hours (Clay, Lingwall, & Stephens, 2012).

A Swiss educator named Johann Heinrich Pestalozzi had a large impact on the educational system in the United States at the turn of the 19th century (Keene, 1982). Pestalozzi advocated for a different approach to education. Rather than treating children like little adults and having them memorize information, Pestalozzi encouraged education to follow children's development. This more child-centered approach included play, group work, music, physical education, and treating children with kindness. He was also a proponent for educating teachers so that they would not be just people who knew facts, reading, and writing, but would also be people who understood how to best educate children using approaches that matched children's natural ways of learning and knowing.

LOWELL MASON AND PUBLIC SCHOOL MUSIC

Fig. 2.1: Lowell Mason.

Lowell Mason, a singing school teacher and church music leader working in Massachusetts, applied Pestalozzi's principles to teaching music to children. When he wrote music lessons, he included questions for the students and exercises for them to do. This made music classes interactive sessions in which, for the first time, the students were active learners. Mason went on to become one of the biggest influences on music education. He co-founded the Boston Academy of Music, which was a private music school, and advocated for vocal music instruction to be included in all public schools (Mark, 2008). The academy became very popular and successful in teaching students how to sing and read music. In 1837, Mason volunteered his time as a music teacher in Boston Public Schools for one year to help show the school board the benefits of vocal music instruction, thereby becoming the first public music educator in the country. In 1838, because of Mason's work at the academy, and the success of his experimental first year regularly teaching vocal music to the children in South Boston's Hawes School, the Boston school board approved the addition of vocal music classes to all of its public schools. Although some public and many private schools in Boston and elsewhere had included music classes before this time, such classes were added by individual school principals or at the instigation of churches, not systematically offered for all children in all schools. The Boston school board was the first in the United States to make music instruction part of the standard public school curriculum (Birge, 1928).

The first public school music classes focused entirely on vocal music. Instrumental music came into school settings after communities heard and got excited by touring bands and orchestras. These touring ensembles were so popular that parents wanted their children to become involved in them as well. Orchestras came first in the public schools, followed by bands (Mark, 2008). In 1896, there were grammar school orchestras in New London, Connecticut, and these also arrived in Hartford, Connecticut, by 1899 (Birge, 1928). Music educator Will Earhart started a high school orchestra in Richmond, Indiana, that met after school hours, but in which students earned high school credit. In 1918, Rochester, New York, was the home of the first supervisor of instrumental music in the country, Joseph Maddy, who convinced George Eastman to donate $10,000 worth of instruments to Rochester-area schools; with this assistance, Maddy created an outstanding instrumental music program (Mark, 2008).

The number of schools offering band and orchestra instruction grew rapidly from 1900 to 1922. This growth was fueled, in part, by economics. The invention and popularity of Ford's affordable Model T car enabled people to travel more easily to find entertainment, so instead of relying on trolley cars to take them to outdoor amusement parks where large concert bands provided music, people drove to clubs where smaller dance bands played swing and Latin music for dancing (Mark, 2008). The success of radio in promoting dance music also contributed to the decline of concert band music's popularity. American musical instrument manufacturers' sales were reduced by the decline of concert bands, so they began to invest in and support school music programs as a growing market by, for example, funding and promoting national school band contests. Both the public and the educational community viewed participation in school bands and orchestras as a form of positive and healthy socializing (for boys, almost exclusively, until the mid-20th century) that supported good citizenship and democracy (Mark, 2008).

The Russians launched *Sputnik I*, the world's first manmade satellite, into orbit in 1957. In the era of the Cold War, this Russian scientific advance had a major influence on the educational system in the United States. The government and citizens of the United States felt that they were falling behind the Russians, and national pride and safety were on the line. Government agencies and the public pushed schools to require more science and math, and public dollars went to more teachers, time, and equipment for these subjects, which left little time or money for the arts. The Cold War era was the first time the federal government became highly involved in education, which had been the purview of the state governments since Massachusetts first established compulsory schooling (Mark, 2008). The federal government made funds available for schools that emphasized those subjects that the government thought would put the United States ahead of Russia and other countries. Although there were many advocates for arts education during this time, the overall national feeling was that by concentrating on the "basics," the United States would become a stronger and more competitive country. The negative effects of the national "back to basics" movement led to the need for advocacy for arts education to remain important in public schools.

ADVOCACY FOR MUSIC EDUCATION

For decades, national music organizations have helped music educators advocate for music's importance in public education. Historically, there have been several different national organizations for teachers, including the National Teachers Association (NTA) and the National Education Association (NEA). During the 1970s, the NEA stopped being an organization and became a labor union so that it could advocate and lobby Congress for better working conditions and compensation for its constituents (Mark & Gary, 2007). For musicians, the Music Teachers National Association (MTNA) was the first of its kind; it mainly concentrated on the needs of private music instructors. Music educators were members of MTNA as well, so there were often disagreements as to the pursuit of the organization. In 1910, the Music Supervisors National Conference was established as an organization dedicated to the promotion of music education for every child (Mark & Gary, 2007). It was renamed the Music Educators National Conference (MENC) in 1934. Over the course of the next several decades, MENC's name suggested that it was simply an event, a conference, and not the national advocacy group for music education. To make a clearer statement for advocacy and to more clearly identify with its purpose, MENC changed its name to the National Association for Music Education (NAfME) in 2011. It is important to note that throughout its history and still today, NAfME advocates not only for music education for every child, but also that qualified music specialists (like you!)—not just any teacher—should teach music in schools.

One of the most important jobs of these national organizations is to advocate not only for their members (music educators), but also for every child in the United States. Having one large organization rather than many small ones gives NAfME a louder and more influential voice in Congress and with school administrators. NAfME provides resources for its members, such as networking opportunities, research and teaching practices journals, and online advocacy guides and forums, and it brings the concerns and accomplishments of music education to a national platform. Having a national organization also serves to legitimize your cause—your national organization has enough influence to have a place at the negotiations table when big decisions regarding education occur.

Figure 2.2 shows an example of a NAfME ad for an annual Capitol Hill advocacy event.

Fig. 2.2: NAfME ad for annual capitol hill advocacy event.

Education does not happen in a vacuum; instead, it happens within, through, and because of all levels of society. As you can see from this brief survey of music education's history, education reflects the society in which it takes place. When a society condones putting its children in the workforce instead of requiring them to be in school, that society does not value highly the learning that school provides. As a society recognizes or endorses the benefits of education, the role of schooling changes. Whether it is preparing citizens for participation in music festivals, or preparing worshippers to sing well in church, or building the United States into a global superpower in science and math, education reflects the values of the people in charge at any given time. When society's values turn "back to basics," subjects like reading, writing, and mathematics get emphasized and arts education suffers (ironically, considering that the most basic educational model, ancient Greece, included music!).

Advocacy for music education begins with the quality of your school music program. The most effective way to advocate for any music program is for that program to succeed as the *community it is in defines it*. Because schools' funding is affected by votes and school boards from the community, it is the community's action that defines

Fig. 2.3: NAfME community advocacy advertisement.

what success is, as well as which musical contributions to the community they value enough to support.

These are some questions to ask yourself as a music educator whose job, and whose program, depends on community support: In what ways have your students' musical activities made a positive difference to your community? Are the students graduating from your program ready to do anything that your community values? Are graduates of your program able to be lifelong musicians in any capacity they want because of having you as a music teacher? Are you serving all students, or only a few who community members believe could afford to get lessons on their own without public funding? Does your program offer anything to your community that your community actually needs or requests (for example, musically honoring veterans or returning soldiers at community events, adding music to community holiday celebrations and thereby bringing more people to downtown businesses to shop, serving at soup kitchens, collecting food bank donations at your concerts, etc.)? Do you schedule concerts without consideration of other community events, such as sports tournaments, major sales dates (Black Friday), hunting seasons, or farm planting and harvesting times? Do you output information only without asking for or listening to community organizations' needs? Do you publicize your students' musical achievements beyond the school newsletters that only parents see? After you establish a successful music program, advocacy is much easier because many people

Fig. 2.4: Waconia High School Marching Band clarinetists performing in parade.

in your community see the value your program adds, and they want that value to continue.

CONCLUSION

This brief overview of the history of music education can help you understand how music came to be part of public schooling. Use this history to inform others who, for example, may not know that music was part of ancient Greek education, and that it has been in U.S. public schools since 1837. Use history as a reference point when discussing current issues. Essential resources, such as funding, class time, rehearsal space, scheduling that allows maximal student participation, and public support, are often at issue in music education. When music educators recognize and use the importance of the historical, educational, and societal contexts in which music education occurs, they increase their abilities to gain essential resources.

REFERENCES

Birge, E. B. (1928). *History of public school music in the United States.* Washington, DC: Music Educators National Conference.

Clay, K., Lingwall, J., & Stephens, M., Jr. (2012). *Do schooling laws matter? Evidence from the introduction of compulsory attendance laws in the United States* (NBER Working Paper No. 18477). Retrieved from http://www.nber.org/papers/w18477

Keene, J. A. (1982). *A history of music education in the United States.* Hanover, NH: University Press of New England.

Mark, M. L. (2008). *A concise history of American music education.* Lanham, MD: Rowman & Littlefield.

Mark, M. L., & Gary, C. L. (2007). *A history of American music education* (3rd ed.). Lanham, MD: Rowman & Littlefield.

Mayer, G. (2010). Child labor in America: History, policy and legislative issues. In I. C. Rivera and N. M. Howard (Eds.), *Child labor in*

America (pp. 37–80). Hauppauge, NY: Nova Science Publishers. [Electronic version]

DISCUSSION QUESTIONS

1. What parallels do you see between what happened to attitudes about music making in ancient Greece and current views of music education?

2. What was Rev. John Tufts's contribution to music education in the United States?

3. How does Lowell Mason's work impact current music education practices and policies?

4. How was Johann Heinrich Pestalozzi's philosophy toward education different from the philosophy of education that was previously used in the United States?

5. What advocacy for music education have you witnessed or participated in? Was it aimed at everyone, or was it mostly effective for those already interested and participating in music?

Image Credits

CHAPTER 3

CHILD DEVELOPMENT

I would like to start talking about children based on what they are *not*.

What children are *not*:

- They are not little adults.
- They are not less intelligent than they will be when they are older, so they do not require that you "dumb down" anything for them.
- They are not empty vessels into which you pour your knowledge.
- They are not blank slates upon which you write.
- They are not sponges that soak up information.

What children *are*:

- They are naturally creative.
- They are naturally curious.
- They have their own set of experiences and preferences.
- They are immature ... they are supposed to be—that's their job.

Fig. 3.1: Children are natural musicians.

Child development is the study of how children develop in particular areas over time. Development is different from, but related to, growth. For example, as children grow, their brains grow (of course), but neural growth is more than just changing size; it involves changing connections, adapting to challenges, and so much more that affects the ways children think and learn at different ages. Children develop socially, educationally, musically, physically, and so on. As you study music education, you will learn about research from theorists who have had a big impact on our understanding of how children learn as they change in their development from birth to young adulthood. Educators apply research in children's development to how they structure their classrooms, curriculum, and assessment, so that students of all ages can learn effectively.

I will discuss a few of the most well-known theorists and the implications that their findings have on our music classrooms. Again, this is just a small sampling of a number of important people, ideas, and best teaching practices in the world of music education.

Children think differently than adults do. They think in a concrete manner, not in an abstract manner as adults do (Piaget & Inhelder, 1969).

Concrete	Abstract

What it is:

It's an awesome moose!

What it means:

Up to interpretation ... it can be anything.

Uses only the information provided:

Children are literal—if I said to get your boots, children would bring only their boots (no clothes, socks, coat, etc.).

Fills in the gaps:

If she's telling me to get my boots, it's cold out. I'll grab my coat while I'm there.

Makes observations:

It's sunny!

Makes conclusions:

I'd better get my sunglasses and sunscreen.

Understanding is tied to context:

I know I have to use my "inside voice" when I am in a store, but no one ever told me to be quiet during worship services ...

Can conserve information when the context changes:

Since I have been told I need to use a respectful, quiet voice when in a store, I know that means any public place has the same rule.

Makes incorrect generalized assumptions

Ex: I am allowed to run after my ball when it rolls away, therefore I can run into the street if my ball rolls into it.

Sees the implications behind actions and events

Ex: Even though my ball is in the street, I could be in serious danger if I ran out to get it.

Action – playing, singing, moving to music.

Musical Notation – reading music, interpreting meaning.

Child development theorists and researchers have found that children begin to think abstractly at different ages, depending on factors, such as the child's cultural and social experience, and the child's experiences with the subject or nature of the abstract thinking needed. Piaget believed children could think abstractly around 11 or 12 years of age, and many theorists agree with the general timing of around sixth grade. Although children can begin to think abstractly around this age, many will still need practice and help to be effective abstract thinkers.

Fig. 3.2: Jean Piaget.

JEAN PIAGET

Jean Piaget (1896–1980) was a Swiss psychologist who developed four stages of child development in which he identified how children matured and progressed through cognitive processing (thinking; Piaget, 1952). They are (with ages):

1. Sensorimotor (0–2)

   Babies see, touch, hear—they have direct experiences through their senses. "This is fuzzy! That's scratchy."

2. Preoperational (2–7)

   Children focus on one aspect at a time—"Moose have antlers, so all animals with antlers must be moose."

3. Concrete operations (7–11)

   Children think in a concrete, systematic, logical manner—"That antlered animal is much smaller than a moose; it must be a male deer."

4. Formal operations (12+)

   Children think abstractly—"What would a moose look like if it were blue and water skiing?"

These four stages may take longer or shorter amounts of time, but children progress through them in order. The point of these stages is to illustrate that children think differently according to their development. Even though a 2-year-old is highly intelligent, that child is still unable to think abstractly. The child will not be able to see consequences of his or her actions. It is not a matter of how smart the child is—the brain is not ready for that kind of thinking yet.

HOWARD GARDNER

Howard Gardner (1943–) is a professor of cognition and education at Harvard University's School of Education. He is best known for his theory of multiple intelligences (1983, 2003), in which he identified eight intelligences. This was groundbreaking work when it first came out. Prior to this theory, if you were a carpenter, you were "good with your hands." If you were a musician, you were "talented"; and if you were an athlete, you were … well … an athlete. With his theory, Gardner changed that perspective to say that you are *intelligent* in those fields. He expanded the definition of intelligence from being good in a very narrow scope (math, taking tests, science, etc.), and led us to think about intelligence from a standpoint of different perspectives. I have put them in the pattern shown in Figure 3.5 to illustrate the fact that none are more important than any other.

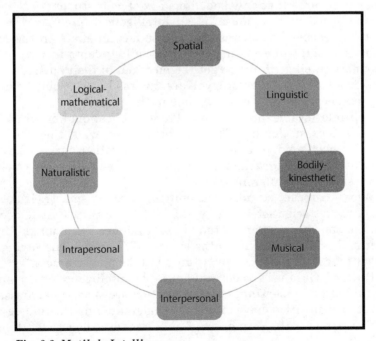

Fig. 3.3: Mutilple Intelligences.

Spatial: Architect, designer, chess player, etc.

Bodily-kinesthetic: Athlete, dancer, etc.

Musical: Musician, conductor, composer, etc.

Linguistic: Writer, journalist, poet, etc.

Logical-mathematical: Mathematician, scientist, etc.

Interpersonal: Coach, motivator, politician

Intrapersonal: This does not correlate with particular professions. People with strong intrapersonal intelligence are self-aware and sensitive to their own feelings and goals.

Naturalistic: You are "in tune" to nature—park rangers, environmentalists, etc.

Reflect on how these attributes of intelligence have far-reaching implications.

 Consider this: You are a school administrator and you need to cut expenses. You have a music program that works with talented students only. *Talented* means that you have a natural ability that not everyone has. If music is not for everyone, and is only for those who are talented, wouldn't you consider saving money in an area that only benefits a few of your students?

Now consider that music is an intelligence. *Intelligence* is the ability to learn—that means that music has an effect on the brain and is important to everyone. You want all students in your school to be more intelligent and to get the most out of their education and brain development; therefore, you are far less likely to cut the music program because it impacts everyone in the school.

Multiple intelligence also has large implications for social justice. Consider mechanics. They are brilliant in what they do—they can take apart engines and put them back together again—they are certainly no less *smart* than musicians or rocket scientists. They are simply smart in a different way.

Why is a rocket scientist the epitome of being smart? "It doesn't take a rocket scientist to figure this out …" means that it doesn't take the smartest person on the planet to figure out a simple thing. What makes rocket scientists the smartest? Why isn't the saying, "It doesn't take a musician …" or "It doesn't take a mechanic …"?

Howard Gardner's theory of multiple intelligences is a major step forward in understanding that intelligence is not a narrow set of skills that you either have or do not. Understanding the unique way people learn is at the very heart of understanding how to teach to all students.

JEROME BRUNER

Jerome Bruner (1915–2016) was a psychologist and research professor at New York University. Bruner (1966) proposed that children use three modes of representation—that is, ways in which children learn information. These modes are

- **Enactive:** action-based (the doing of ...)

  - Children up to age 1

  - A child would represent something big by holding out his or her arms.

  - Musically, a child would sing or play music without knowledge or awareness of notation.

- **Iconic:** concrete images (pictures of things), language

  - Ages 1–6

  - Visual examples help children learn. Children this age understand that a picture of a ball means "ball" and signifies the round thing they enjoy chasing; they learn that pictures of things *stand for* things.

  - Invented music notation: Children can notate music by drawing or following pictures or figures that correspond to the claps in a rhythm pattern.

- **Symbolic:** abstract symbols (i.e., written words and notation)

  - Ages 7 and up

  - Written words and notation can help children understand music, and children can explain or create music using these symbols.

  - Children can learn and gain meaning from music's standard notation, which is symbolic of sounds, silences, durations, note groupings, and simultaneities (harmony).

LEV VYGOTSKY

Lev Vygotsky (1896–1934) was born in Russia. Although he never pursued a degree in psychology (his degree was in law), his theories of child development remain very influential.

Fig. 3.4: Lev Vygotsky.

Unlike Piaget, who believed that the main element in child development was cognition, Vygotsky believed that social interactions were the most influential factors in children's learning. He suggested that children actually develop more quickly through their social interactions. He developed the idea of the zone of proximal development (ZPD; 1978). The ZPD is the difference between what children can understand and accomplish on their own and what children can come to understand and accomplish with the help of more capable peers or a competent adult. The ZPD is significant for teaching because it explains the importance of the social aspects of learning. It also stresses the individuality of each child's development, because children's zones vary according to their experiences and the social and cultural settings in which they learn. Vygotsky believed that development was far more complicated than simply passing an age—he believed children learned best by constructing their own knowledge (by experimenting, playing, etc.) and that no situation could be removed from the social context. For example, you cannot separate yourself from the social context of your life. You are a product of the people around you, the society you live in, and the world as a whole. These social influences have an impact on how you learn.

CHILDREN'S MUSICAL DEVELOPMENT

After reading about theories of children's cognitive development, you may be wondering (I hope you are!) if children's musical cognition and activity develop similarly. Research reveals that there *are* predictable age- and context-related developmental shifts in children's musical thinking and doing.

Singing Development

Children are natural singers. They sing when they play, they sing their own created songs, and they sing along with television shows, commercials, the radio, and so on. In fact, if you listen to a young child for just an hour, you will probably hear that child sing. As music teachers, we are charged with the responsibility of helping children sing tunefully, and with vocal

Fig. 3.5: 18-month-old Maya singing spontaneously.

health, an expansive repertoire of songs. We must choose music that is appropriate in range, tessitura, and content to enable children to sing musically, and we must serve as excellent and accurate vocal models.

First, let's address the difference between a child's range and the tessitura of a song. *Range* can refer to the pitches a child is capable of singing—the range between the lowest and highest notes children are likely to be able to sing at specific ages without damaging their vocal mechanism. *Range* can also refer to the range of a song—the distance between the lowest and highest pitches of a given song.

Tessitura, on the other hand, refers to the part of the range in which most pitches of a song lie. A song's tessitura affects the difficulty and vocal stress involved in singing it. For example, imagine that a song has a range that spans from middle C to the G above the treble staff; however, its tessitura, the majority of the song, lies between the first line E and an octave above that. Although the range of that song would require you to sing higher and lower than those octave Es, the majority of the piece would lie within an octave. The E-octave, therefore, would be the *tessitura* for the song.

Tuneful singing involves coordination of physiological factors that include posture, breath, larynx, and listening with psychological factors of pitch awareness and perception, known as *audiation* (Gordon, 1999). Children may naturally match pitches well by first or second grade, but most of those who struggle to do so can improve with appropriate systematic instruction (Phillips, 2014). Research indicates that children's singing development involves phases or styles of vocalization that begin with words often repeated in singsong or chant-like style and with vocal swoops and imitation of sounds

(Gordon, 2013; Rutkowski, 1997; Welch, 1986). Children's pitch matching shifts among states of matching the contour of melodies without complete pitch accuracy, matching phrases or motives within melodies accurately but shifting among keys, and matching smaller intervals more accurately than larger intervals, such as the octave (Rutkowski, 1997; Welch, 1986).

To enable children to sing tunefully, teachers must be accurate singing models in the children's vocal ranges (Dickey, 1992). Male music teachers need to teach young children using their falsetto. This greatly increases a child's ability to match pitch. Female music teachers need to teach young children without vibrato, again, for the best pitch matching. Children's singing needs to be clear and relatively light, so modeling that way is very important. It also helps maintain the vocal health of both teachers and students. Shouting, singing for prolonged periods of time in the chest voice, and using other unhealthy singing techniques can lead to prolonged vocal damage.

Rhythmic Development

Children's understanding, perception, and performance of rhythm also changes in predictable ways as they grow and participate in musical activities. Humans' sense of hearing begins to function about three months before children are born. Infants in the first months of life respond to changes in patterns, meters, and tempos (Tan, Pfordresher, & Harré, 2010). Toddlers sway, step from foot to foot, and bounce in response to rhythms and music as early as their first year, and most children are able to coordinate listening with their actions to match, pat (with both hands), and chant the beat and rhythm patterns in different tempos by first grade (Moorehead & Pond, 1978). Children prefer, initiate, and match faster tempos than adults do (Drake, Jones, & Baruch, 2000).

REFERENCES

Bruner, J. (1966). *Toward a theory of instruction*. Cambridge, MA: Harvard University Press.

Dickey, M. R. (1992). A review of research on modeling in music teaching and learning. *Bulletin of the Council for Research in Music Education, 113*, 27–40.

Drake, C., Jones, M. R., & Baruch, C. (2000). The development of rhythmic attending in auditory sequences: Attunement, referent period, focal attending. *Cognition, 77*(3), 251–288.

Gardner, H. (1983). *Frames of mind: The theory of multiple intelligences.* New York, NY: Basic Books.

Gardner, H. (2003, April 12). *Multiple intelligence after 20 years.* Paper presented at the meeting of the American Educational Research Association, Chicago, Illinois.

Gordon, E. E. (1999). *All about audiation and music aptitudes.* Chapel Hill, NC: Hinshaw.

Gordon, E. E. (2013). *Music learning theory for newborn and young children.* Chicago, IL: GIA Music.

Moorehead, G. E., & Pond, D. (1978). *Music of young children.* Santa Barbara, CA: Pillsbury Foundation.

Piaget, J. (1952). *The psychology of intelligence* (M. Percy & D. E. Berlyne, Trans.). London, UK: Routledge & Kegan Paul.

Piaget, J., & Inhelder, B. (1969). *The psychology of the child.* New York, NY: Basic Books.

Phillips, K. H. (2014). *Teaching kids to sing* (2nd ed.). Boston, MA: Schirmer, Cengage Learning.

Rutkowski, J. (1997). The nature of children's singing voices: Characteristics and assessment. In B. A. Roberts (Ed.), *The phenomenon of singing* (pp. 201–209). St. John's, NF: Memorial University Press.

Tan, S., Pfordresher, P., & Harré, R. (2010). *Psychology of music: From sound to significance.* New York, NY: Psychology Press.

Vygotsky, L. S. (1978). *Mind in society: The development of higher mental processes.* Cambridge, MA: Harvard University Press.

Welch, G. (1986). Children's singing: A developmental continuum of ability. *Journal of Research in Singing, 9*(2), 49–56.

DISCUSSION QUESTIONS

1. How are Piaget and Vygotsky's theories similar, and how do they differ?

2. Give your own specific musical and nonmusical examples of Bruner's enactive, iconic, and symbolic modes of representation.

3. Think of people you know who have a strong intelligence in each of Gardner's eight intelligences. How would you teach each of them something new? Would you alter your instruction based on their strengths?

Image Credits

- Fig. 3.1: Photo by Laura M. Dornberger.

- Source: https://commons.wikimedia.org/wiki/File:Bigbullmoose.jpg.

- Source: https://commons.wikimedia.org/wiki/File:3200x2400-texture-pd2001.jpg.

- Fig. 3.2: From the Michiganensian Yearbook (1968), p. 91. Public Domain.

- Fig. 3.3: Photo by Laura M. Dornberger.

- Source: https://pixabay.com/en/frog-green-animal-amphibian-48234/.

- Fig. 3.4: Copyright © by The Vygotsky Project, (CC BY-SA 3.0) at https://commons.wikimedia.org/wiki/File:Lev_Vygotsky_1896-1934.jpg.

CHAPTER 4

SOCIETY'S INFLUENCE ON MUSIC EDUCATION

Sociology is very important in music education because music is such an integral part of human society. Think about all the different ways you hear music on a typical day. Music is a part of advertising, television and movies, sporting events, retail stores and restaurants—it is an ever-present function of our lives. In a larger sense, music is also a part of our culture. For example, we use folk music, spirituals, and ritualistic music to remember and to hand down traditions and knowledge. We also use music to identify ourselves—from national anthems to team songs to fans of a particular artist, group, or genre.

POSITIONALITY

It is important to realize music's deep cultural roots as we enter a classroom in a position of authority. Teachers can purposefully or accidentally exclude entire musical cultures from school music study because they are not familiar with them or do not value them as highly as other music. This power we teachers have over the choices of music and musical experiences requires a discussion of positionality. The position in society that teachers have is of crucial importance in our teaching. As a teacher, your personal perspective on life, on music, on students' behaviors—on *everything*—enters the classroom with you. Your knowledge is limited by that perspective. In other words, you cannot choose to teach what you do not know. Your race, gender identity, socioeconomic background, primary language, and familial experiences contribute to your perspective as you enter a classroom as a teacher, and your perspective naturally biases your thinking and greatly impacts each and every student you teach.

The first step in becoming a mature and relevant teacher for every student in your classes is to acknowledge the role this positionality has in your teaching.

Based on your experiences and education, you likely have already begun to decide what musical and nonmusical content you think will be important to teach. The music you think is important—or, more meaningfully, the music you do *not* think is important to include in your classes and ensembles—will shape your students' experiences in your program. Although it is tempting to assume that new teachers walk into the classroom bias-free, sociology studies (Doyle, 2014, Hess, 2015) show that it is more likely that each of us brings specific expectations for our students and ourselves with us into the classroom. You need to be aware of your positionality in order to work effectively within the social context in which you find yourself teaching, and to meet your students' learning needs, rather than to expect the social norms of the school and community to conform to your perspective.

Make notes of your answers as you ask yourself these questions:

What Will Your Students Do With the Information They Learn in Your Class?

Is your intention for your students to go on to study music when they leave your classroom? Or is your intention for them to be able to participate in music, in some way, for the rest of their lives? Do you want your students to be better people because of your instruction, and you don't care as much (or at all) what they do musically in their future lives? Do you want them to somehow change the world for the better based on the experiences you have provided?

Where Do You See Your Students Using Music in Their Lives Outside of Your Classroom and Schooling?

Do you want students to be able to play chamber music on their own or to be able to start a rock band? Do you expect they will know how to compose, transpose, and find music they can play in such groups in stores or online? Do you see some students as being consumers of music and others as being performers? Should everyone be a performer? Should everyone who learns to perform in school sing or play traditional Western art instruments found in bands and orchestras? Do you imagine including keyboard and guitar in your program? What about instruments from other cultures or inexpensive folk instruments, such as harmonica or washtub bass?

What Do You Want Students to Know and Be Able to Do as a Result of Being in Your Class?

What will your students be able to do that they wouldn't be able to do had they never taken your class? Is playing or listening to genres of music they don't usually listen to enough to musically educate someone? Does playing Bach and having students answer questions automatically lead to "music appreciation"?

What Will Your "Ideal" Student Choose to Do?

Is your ideal student one who goes on to become a music teacher just like you? Would you be most proud of a student who goes on to study music? Would you rather your students be able to read music, or be able to play by ear, or ... ? When your ideal student becomes an adult, would he or she attend live performances, buy recorded music, compose music for family video presentations, or play or sing in community groups? What kind of music teaching should you do to make sure that students can realize these ideals?

What Kind of People Do You Find Difficult to Be Around?

What kind of person annoys you immediately? You will be teaching hundreds and hundreds of unique students who will have a wide variety of strengths, weaknesses, needs, viewpoints, personalities, and so on. You will be colleagues with hundreds of different teachers,  many of whom may not value music as a school subject or an academic pursuit, yet you will need to respect and value their roles within your school and your shared students' learning. If you choose instead to alienate yourself and your music program from the school and community, you will risk having the availability of music classes in the school schedule compromised, your school purchasing budget reduced, and your position—perhaps even the entire music program—cut because its relevance to the greater community is questionable. You also will interact with countless parents and families who will have a wide range of opinions and expectations for their children, and for you as their children's teacher. Your job will be to teach *all* your students equally well, to collaborate and work successfully with all your colleagues, and to communicate and maintain professional integrity with parents and administrators, whether or not their personalities and beliefs match your likes and dislikes.

Who Is the Most Important Person in a Classroom?

Is it the teacher? Are teachers the center of the classroom—beacons of knowledge and skill who illuminate those who do not yet possess that knowledge? Or are the students the center of the classroom? If students are the most important people in the classroom, what role does the teacher take? When you teach, will you make an exact plan of everything you will do that day, or will you set aside time in your lessons to find out what the students need that day?

What Kind of Music Do You Think Is the Best?

Do you consider it to be your job to educate all students on the beauty and importance of Western art music, or popular music, or music from different cultures and countries? Do you find country music to be less educational than classic rock music? Is there a genre of music or even a piece of music that you think everyone should learn, regardless of their background?

When you start to honestly consider and answer these questions, you will start to become more aware of your positionality, and a clearer picture of what you expect out of your teaching career will emerge. Through reflection on your answers, you can better consider what teaching settings you might find comfortable and what kinds of students' values you will find easy to relate to. Some of you will feel very well suited to teaching in public schools, whereas others will feel more suited to teach at a university or conservatory.

SOCIOLOGY AND SCHOOLS

The questions above that concern your positionality are designed to introduce you to some sociological issues you will face as an educator. As a music teacher, you must know about the sociology of education, because your job blends the traditions of music study, listening, and creating with the tradition of socially mandated education (Froelich, 2007). While you study to earn a university music degree, you likely will increase your knowledge of Western art music history, literature, and performance practice. You will study piano, singing, music theory, and, of course, musical performance. However, this in-depth study of music as a performance art may distance you from the work of school systems in which you expect to teach. School policies in the United States often concern (a) the need for *all* children, not just nondisabled students in school districts with strong financial resources, to gain maximum benefits from education (evidenced by federal and state initiatives, such as "Race to the Top," "No Child Left Behind," and "School Choice"), (b) proof of and accountability for students' learning of the content and skills society deems relevant (evidenced by mandated standardized testing, annual student learning objective tests, and comparisons of U.S. student scores with scores from other nations' children), and (c) funding for and control of schools (property tax funds, state funding formulas, Common Core State Standards, Goals 2000: Educate America). It might surprise you to know that teachers of English, math, social studies, and so on experience similar stress reconciling the traditional values in their areas of study with the constraints of public schooling. Those who teach must balance the love they have for their subject with their knowledge about learning and teach with awareness of, and respect for, the social contexts in which they and their students live and learn.

Classes, ensembles, schools, and communities are rife with social contexts that affect students' music learning. Consider the many groups to which your students may belong, with varying levels of complexity and interest: family, gender, ethnicity, race, language, faith, culture, peer groups (including gangs, cliques, sports teams, sports fans, musical artist or band followers, Scouts, and many more). Social group interactions include a range of roles—leaders, followers, bullies, victims, watchers, informers, and so on—and most social settings involve hierarchical interactions among the people in them. Consider, for example, the hierarchical nature of most school environments: Students turn in work to, and receive assessment from, teachers, who turn in lesson plans as well as students' grades and test scores to parents and administrators, who use these scores to assess teachers as well as students. Administrators submit school data reports to school boards, who use them to assess administrators' school leadership (as well as teachers and students). School boards publish school statistics, test scores, and budgets, which taxpayers and state education officials use to rate schools' success or failure, which is also publicized in the media, where it may be noted by major employers, who communicate their expectations for the education of the work force to politicians, who solicit votes from taxpayers, who send their children to school.

SOCIAL CONTEXTS AND SOCIAL CAPITAL

Social factors often weigh heavily in students' decisions to take or to opt out of elective music courses because they impact students' perceptions of the place music could have in their lives, as a part of their school day, as a way they could stand out or fit in, as something the people they know do or do not do, or as something they must do, are prohibited from doing, or have the choice to do.

Social factors impact the support children have from home in terms of reminders to practice, the ability to participate in ensembles outside of the school day, or the funds to rent an instrument.

One sociological concept music teachers find useful for getting the best outcomes from social factors is the concept of social capital (Putnam, 2001). According to Putnam, *social capital* consists of "connections among individuals—social networks and the norms of reciprocity and trustworthiness that arise from them" (2001, p. 19). In settings with high social capital, people are better able to resolve problems that affect their groups, business and social transactions improve, information needed for achieving community goals flows productively, and individuals gain awareness of ways in which their fates connect. Socially excluded persons and marginalized groups, such as ethnic minorities, individuals with certain disabilities or health concerns, and those who live in poverty, lack the social capital needed to thrive in society. However, involvement in groups that make, create, and listen to music can build social capital by focusing students' attention on collaborative efforts to reach shared goals and valuing connections among group members (harmony—literally; Wright, 2012). Think of the social connections you made from participating in school music groups. Unfortunately, participation in music groups can also solidify exclusion and inequality when only those students with social capital participate in them. It is up to you, as a future teacher, to lead music classes and make room for group music making that appeal to and engage the full range of students in your school setting (Wright, 2012).

AGENCY AND MINDSET

Music teachers can also benefit from understanding the sociological construct of agency. Sociologists use the word *agency* to refer to a person's capacity to take voluntary action. More specifically, Bruner (1996) defines the agency students need as a "sense that one can initiate and carry out activities on one's own' linked to aspiration, confidence, optimism, and know-how" (pp. 35–36). In order to learn, your students need to actively attempt to understand and to do music. Some of your students will find music easier than others do. Music making, whether performing, composing, improvising, or discussing listening preferences, involves your students taking risks and showing vulnerability (Wiggins, 2011). You probably are aware of feeling vulnerable yourself when you perform, improvise, or compose. When learners allow themselves to be vulnerable, and their efforts result in success, understanding, knowledge, and acceptance, they gain more agency in music making, and in their lives as a whole. However, when they allow themselves to be vulnerable and they experience

betrayal, feel wounded, or attacked, they develop resistance and withdraw from musical activity to protect themselves. Their agency in music learning diminishes. As Wiggins explains,

"While there are some unavoidably stressful aspects of music making and learning—and we do want to help our students learn to cope—we certainly have within our control the capacity to reduce the amount of stress and adversity involved in these settings" (2011, p. 364).

Teachers can reduce stress and adversity by providing and soliciting from students honest constructive feedback, and by setting classroom and rehearsal hall environments where students are safe to take appropriate musical risks. How many times have you heard conductors say, "Take a deeper breath, set your embouchure/vocal placement/thumb position, and try again for that high note!" (I feel vulnerable just describing that scene!) Yet students can develop a sense of purpose when they discover that their music making can improve when they accept and apply constructive feedback. The knowledge that one can get better makes the risks involved worthwhile. Stepping out of sociology for a moment and into psychology, teachers who give accurate feedback and consistent messages that failure is reasonable because it can be the path to real improvement can help students develop a growth mindset instead of a fixed mindset (Dweck, 2006/2016).

Some of the most talented students in your programs may have a fixed mindset, which includes the belief that talented people must prove themselves by succeeding without requiring much effort, and that, because of their talent, they should not fail. When these students make mistakes or fail to perform well, fixed mindset learners tend to become angry and frustrated and to blame factors out of their control, like the contest judges, cheaters, or conditions in the performance room. This is a fixed mindset—"fixed" because it is a belief that people have talent, ability, or intelligence in fixed unchangeable quantities, and that when people struggle, practice, fail, or make mistakes, it indicates weakness and lack of talent. Research indicates that people who have a fixed mindset avoid doing what could actually increase their success because they believe that, for example, practicing diligently and regularly would essentially prove they lacked talent (Dweck, 2006/2016).

In contrast, students who have a growth mindset believe that their capabilities will grow with effort. Challenges interest them because they believe they will learn and grow from them.

In her studies, psychologist Carol Dweck engaged adolescent students who earned poor grades and who expressed negative attitudes about learning and school in workshops that teach growth mindset and its application to schoolwork. The workshops began by explaining to students that research in neural development has taught us that intelligence is not something that is unchangeable, and that, in fact, the brain makes more connections, grows, and becomes "smarter" the more you challenge it (Dweck, 2006/2016, pp. 453–455). Dweck and her team members were surprised to hear one of the most school-resistant students respond, with tears in his eyes, "You mean, I don't have to be dumb?" (p. 455). Music is one of the subject areas that students, parents, teachers, and community members most often believe to be talent-based. However, genes and environment *cooperate* as we learn and grow. The brain *changes* and adapts and improves itself. Neuroscientist Gilbert Gottlieb wrote that genes *require* input from the environment to work properly (as cited in Dweck, 2006/2016, p. 17). It is urgent that music teachers consistently inform students, colleagues, and the public of the capacity that all of us have for musical growth. There are genetic differences among us that affect our human strengths and weaknesses, but our brains respond to challenges with learning and growth.

HIDDEN CURRICULUM

A final sociological concept to consider is known as the hidden curriculum (Froehlich, 2007). To understand hidden curriculum, you first need to know what a curriculum is. *Curriculum* is a term used in education to describe the content and specifications of a course of study (Wallace, 2015). In most states, schools must maintain publicly available documentation of their curricula, which list the goals, objectives, standards, and content that students are to learn in each school year in each subject area. New York's state requirements for schools, for example, include more than 20 iterations of the word "curriculum" or its variants (New York State Education Department, 2015).

Now that you know that a school's formal curriculum specifies what students will learn each year in each subject area, you can think about what students could systematically learn in school informally or implicitly, and what is excluded from the formal curriculum. It is assumed that things that are omitted from the curriculum are not worthy of study, or not *as* worthy of study as the things included in the curriculum. Knowledge, skills, or attitudes that students learn from schooling that are outside of or omitted from the curriculum are known as the *hidden curriculum* (Wallace, 2015), sometimes divided into the implicit curriculum and the null curriculum (Ebert, Ebert & Bentley, 2011).

The hidden curriculum may have positive influence. For example, teachers may model and reinforce positive and ethical behaviors that promote effort and cooperation among students. However, hidden curriculum more often is cited as a source of negative messages. For example, Haberman's (1999) study of the 120 largest U.S. school districts indicated that schools' hidden curricula taught students habits that would lead to failure in their future as workers. He questioned acceptance of students' excuses for missed work and tardiness, for example, which would lead to their being fired in a workplace. He questioned separating students who disliked each other instead of rewarding cooperation among students who disagree, which is another behavior required for success in the workplace.

Music teachers, like all other teachers, need to consider what messages they teach students through their choice of musical content, class activities, room and rehearsal organization, rules, and teaching methods. For example, in the positionality quiz at the beginning of this chapter, you answered a number of questions about what kind of music you think is the best, and about your expectations for teaching various genres of music. The music you choose to teach in your program will be part of your formal curriculum. Any genres or cultural music you leave out of your curriculum will be part of your hidden curriculum, because your students will tacitly assume that you do not find that music worthy of study. You may feel that message is appropriate; however, you must also consider the repercussions of leaving out, for example, music that your students like and purchase, and that their families and friends prefer. Students may opt into or out of paying attention in your classes, much like you might respond to music playing in stores or restaurants you pass by, choosing to spend your money where the music matches your preference or mood.

If you believe it is important to include only art music
in your formal curriculum,
what steps can you take to
send the message that this
music can appeal to everyone?
According to the 2015 Arts
Data Profile, a national survey of public participation in
the arts distributed and pub-
lished by the National Endowment for the Arts (2015), the national
percentage of adults who attended a classical concert was 8.8%,
and only 8.1% of the population reported attending a jazz event in
2015. These statistics clearly indicate that, despite generations of
Western art-based school music education, relatively few Americans
choose to attend classical and jazz music events. Does this mean
music teachers should abandon teaching art music? Of course not,
but it does mean that music teachers who aspire to promote the
"understanding and making of music by all," which is the vision
statement of the National Association for Music Education (NAfME,
2015), must take steps to make both the curriculum and the hidden
curriculum diverse and inclusive of all students.

Music education researcher and professor Jacqueline Kelly-
McHale (2016) suggests that you can make your program more
diverse by making your teaching culturally responsive, by enabling
your students to study, perform, and discuss music that is culturally
relevant *to them*. Draw connections between music of the past and
current music to which your students relate. Include in your program
opportunities for students to learn guitar, electric bass, drum set,
keyboard, and to sing and perform in rock groups or in other popular styles. Make room in your program for informal music learning
options, such as Musical Futures (n.d.; www.musicalfutures.org),
that interest and involve all students, especially those who do not
learn well in formal lessons in music making.

CONCLUSION

In considering the effects that positionality, social contexts, social
capital, agency, mindset and hidden curriculum have on music education, you are beginning to understand the importance of studies
in educational sociology. When teachers read and do sociological
research, and apply it to their practice, they engage their students

in the most current, effective, inclusive, and potentially successful learning contexts and experiences.

REFERENCES

Bruner, J. S. (1996). *The culture of education.* Cambridge, MA: Harvard University Press.

Doyle, J. (2014). Predictors of culturally relevant attitudes and expectations of urban music teachers in the USA. *Music Education Research, 16*(4), 436–453.

Dweck, C. S. (2016). *Mindset: The new psychology of success* [iBooks version]. Retrieved from https://itunes.apple.com/us/book/mindset/id422549774?mt=11 (Original work published 2006)

Ebert, E. S., II, Ebert, C., & Bentley, M. L. (2011). *The educator's field guide: From organization to assessment (and everything in between).* Thousand Oaks, CA: Corwin Press.

Froehlich, H. C. (2007). *Sociology for music teachers: Perspectives for practice.* New York, NY: Taylor & Francis.

Haberman, M. (1999). The anti-learning curriculum of urban schools, part 2: The solution. *Kappa Delta Pi Record 35*(2), 71–74. doi: 10.1080/00228958.1999.10518420

Hess, J. (2015). Upping the "anti-": The value of an anti-racist theoretical framework in music education. *Action, Criticism, & Theory in Music Education 14*(1), 66–92. Retrieved from act.maydaygroup.org/articles/Hess14_1.pdf

Kelly-McHale, J. (2016, February 12). Why music education needs to incorporate more diversity. *The Conversation US.* Retrieved from https://theconversation.com/why-music-education-needs-to-incorporate-more-diversity-53789

Musical Futures. (n.d.). *Training, resources, and community for informal music learning and non-formal music teaching.* Retrieved January 7, 2017, from https://www.musicalfutures.org/who-we-are

National Association for Music Education. (2015). *Mission and goals: NAfME strategic plan (2016–2021).* Retrieved January 7, 2017, from https://www.nafme.org/about/mission-and-goals

National Endowment for the Arts. (2015). *Arts data profile #5 (January 2015)—States of engagement: Arts participation by U.S. geography.* Retrieved January 7, 2017, from https://www.arts.gov/artistic-fields/research-analysis/arts-data-profiles/arts-data-profile-5

New York State Education Department. (2015). Part 100.2: General school requirements. *Part 100 regulations.* Retrieved January, 17, 2016, from https://www.p12.nysed.gov/part100/pages/1002.html

Putnam, R. D. (2001). *Bowling alone: The collapse and revival of American community.* New York, NY: Simon and Schuster.

Wallace, S. (Ed.). (2015). *A dictionary of education* (2nd ed.). Oxford, UK: Oxford University Press. Retrieved January 7, 2017, from https://www.oxfordreference.com/view/10.1093/acref/9780199679393.001.0001/acref-9780199679393-e-236

Wiggins, J. (2011). Keynote from 2011 RIME Conference, April 12–16: Vulnerability and agency in being and becoming a musician. *Music Education Research, 13*(4), 355–367.

Wright, R. (2012). Music education and social transformation: Building social capital through music. *Canadian Music Educator 53*(3), 12–13.

DISCUSSION QUESTIONS

1. Consider the kind of environment in which you grew up. Are you most comfortable with similar situations or different ones? In what kinds of situations are you most worried or uncomfortable?

2. Think about the people who were in elementary and middle school music groups with you. Consider those who did not continue in music making the way you did in high school and beyond. What reasons did these peers give for discontinuing music classes? Can you think of any social factors that might have affected their decision to stop taking music classes?

3. Describe an instance in which you or someone you know used to their advantage the social capital they gained in a music setting. For example, my grandfather played drum set in a small band with his friends when he was in high school (in the early 20th century!). The band played in a local dance

club, and as is true in most clubs, the dancing went late into the evening hours. My grandfather therefore found it difficult to make it to his early class on time the next morning. One night while he was playing in the band, he noticed that his first-hour teacher was among the dancers and revelers at the club. In those days, teachers were under strict codes of conduct (even more strict than now, when your careless social media post can result in censure). Because the teacher saw her student, my grandfather, at the club (and because she knew he saw her in this socially questionable setting), she allowed him to be tardy to morning classes without penalty after that night. *Both* the teacher and my grandfather used the social capital they shared in that club music setting.

4. Whenever you use music to show yourself or others your personality, you use music much like you select an outfit to wear, choose to style your hair (or not!), or change your speech to match the listener's age or the setting. Music is part of your *agency*, your way of acting on and in the world. List three ways you used music this week to change your environment to your liking, show someone else what you were thinking, pump up your exercise, change your mood, and so forth.

5. Reflect on your experience as a music learner in school. Choose one of your music teachers to consider more carefully. List three kinds of music, musical knowledge, or musical activity you remember learning/doing in that teacher's classes or ensembles. Were the things that you remember learning part of the teacher's formal curriculum or the hidden curriculum? Can you think of consistent ideals the teacher communicated that were outside of music learning and, therefore, were part of the hidden curriculum?

Image Credits

-   Copyright © by Depositphotos/vitchananphoto.
-   Copyright © by Depositphotos/andreync.
-   Copyright © by Depositphotos/racorn.
-   Copyright © by Depositphotos/Voyagerix.
-   Copyright © by Depositphotos/natursports.
-   Copyright © by Shutterstock Images LLC/Aysezgicmeli.
-   Copyright © by Depositphotos/poznyakov.

CHAPTER 5

EDUCATIONAL PSYCHOLOGY

Educational psychology studies how people (with all their histories and abilities) learn something in particular physical and social settings.

—Anita Woolfolk (cited in Shaughnessy, 2004, p. 161)

It is easy to gloss over the key ideas in this concise definition packed with significant terms. As you reread the definition, underline the verbs, circle the nouns, and note anything that surprised you or caught your attention.

Finished? Woolfolk's definition states that:

Educational psychology <u>studies how</u>

"people"

     with all their "histories" and "abilities"

learn "something"

     in particular physical "settings"

       in particular social "settings."

What "histories" and "abilities" might students in third-grade general music classes have, and how might their histories and abilities differ from those of students in a high school chorus? Which aspects of learners' histories do teachers need to consider? Do students' family

values and experiences affect their music learning? Does their experience with music outside of class affect their learning inside of class? Do students' cultural backgrounds affect their learning? Have research studies indicated that some teaching methods are more effective than others?

How did your histories and abilities affect your music learning during your pre-college years? Did members of your family help you find time to practice (or *insist* that you practice), drive you to or attend performances, invest family funds in your music study, comment on your improvement, or show pride in your musical achievements? Or, was your musical interest in conflict with your family's values? Did you excel in music despite misunderstanding, confusion, or lack of interest from your family? Were you aware of ways your family's interests in your music study differed from the family involvement of other students with whom you went to school?

Whether present and supportive, negative, or uninterested, it is likely that your history with the people you call family, especially with parents, affected your music learning (McPherson, 2009). However, family is only one aspect of your personal history that affects music learning. Others are the culture(s) with which you identify, your participation in religious activity that involves, requires, or forbids you from making or listening to certain music, your history of seeing and hearing live or recorded music, your history moving to music in dance classes, marching, gaming....

Imagine how unique the histories and abilities of the many children you will teach will be! And now, consider that no one of your future students will have history that is *exactly* like yours. Educational psychology research indicates that each of us builds, from personal experience and observation, beliefs about how teaching and learning work (Bruner, 1996). People naturally internalize deeply the learning paths that work well for them so that they can call up those paths and succeed over and over when they face new challenges. However, your learning successes worked for you, in part, because of your personal learning history, your musical abilities, your environment, your culture, your school, and your community. Jerome Bruner (1996) called this experience-based understanding of learning "folk psychology," because, like other kinds of folklore, it is knowledge based on a combination of experience and tradition instead of on systematic study of a broad range of people and contexts. Bruner and others (Box, Skoog, & Dabbs, 2015; Lee & Johnson, 2007; Li, 2003) found that students and teachers are influenced by folk pedagogy, which is teaching based on your personal experience, instead of teaching based on a scientifically investigated understanding of people's learning.

As you move from being a student to being a teacher, you need to rely less on your personal history—your folk pedagogy—and rely more on the learning theories, teaching approaches, and research findings that could work for your *students*. Educational psychology uses social science experimentation and theorizing to systematically study how people with various histories and abilities learn. Because it is so important for teachers to read and be able to use research, most U.S. states require students learning to be teachers to study educational psychology and to apply research to their teaching.

You have considered the first part of Woolfolk's definition of educational psychology, but what about the last part, which states that its studies are of learning in "particular physical and social settings" (as cited in Shaughnessy, 2004, p. 161)? Take a few minutes to list some of the physical and social settings in which you learned music ... For example, you may have learned music through preparing for competitions, auditions, or adjudications. You may have studied music formally at summer music camps, informally through playing by ear with friends in someone's basement, or both formally and informally. You may have discovered many musical techniques by experimenting and practicing long hours by yourself.

Educational psychology studies indicate that different physical and social settings affect learning. You probably already know whether your musicianship grows fastest when you practice in a socially interactive setting, like an ensemble rehearsal, or when you practice in a socially introverted setting alone and focused within yourself. You may be surprised at psychological research findings that professional musicians have higher levels of introversion, independence, and ability to resist social pressure than do amateur musicians (Arshava & Kutepova-Bredun, 2015). Tests of

Fig. 5.1: Engage learners in creativity related to authentic local and global issues.

musicians' personalities indicate tendencies toward anxiety, especially toward anxiety associated with performing musically, and toward psychological androgyny (Kemp, 1985). You may be considering whether or not your personality and learning preferences match some of these characteristics. That is worthwhile thinking, because you must know yourself, your personality, to make sure you offer students *more* than your preferred ways of learning. As a teacher, you will be most comfortable teaching students whose personalities and learning styles match yours. Part of your education to become a teacher will be learning to teach to a wide range of personalities and in different learning settings.

RESEARCH OR OPINION?

Educational research enables teachers to separate fact from fiction. Teachers, professors, and public education agencies all over the world conduct and publish research studies to generate, compare, and test educational theories, teaching practices, learning processes, and teacher education. Read the list of possible research findings below and decide whether you think each statement is research-supported *fact* or commonly believed *fiction*:

1. Violent behaviors are rising in U.S. high schools.

2. Only children are more likely than children with siblings to be self-centered, disadvantaged, and socially isolated.

3. Teachers' enthusiasm for subject matter and for their students positively affect students' learning.

4. High school students whose friends are low academic achievers tend to become less motivated to succeed in school and, over time, to prefer alternate activities that match their peers' beliefs.

5. Adolescent children's ability to play instruments and to sing affects their self-esteem more than their ability to read music does.

6. Parents' expectations for and valuing of their children's musical studies are key to children's success or failure.

Let's see how your perceptions measure up to current research:

"Violent behaviors are rising in U.S. high schools." False. According to the national *Youth Risk Behavior Survey* (CDC, 2015), which is collected by the Centers for Disease Control and Prevention to monitor risk behaviors that contribute to leading causes of death in the United States, incidences of students carrying weapons or being threatened with weapons while at school, participating in fights at school, staying home because they felt unsafe at school, or being bullied at school either decreased or remained the same from 2009 through 2015. School violence is newsworthy and terrible. The tragic impact of school violence can lead to the misperception that it is increasing, when measurements indicate the opposite to be true.

Are only children disadvantaged social isolates because of self-centeredness? No. Research indicates that this unfortunate and widely held belief is a myth. A review comparing the results of more than 140 studies comparing only children with children from small, medium, and large families found no significant differences between only children and children with siblings on measures of maturity, self-control, cooperativeness, social participation, and peer popularity (Polit & Falbo, 1987).

Does teachers' enthusiasm for subject matter and for their students positively affect students' learning? Yes! Researchers Joyce Fleck Long and Anita Woolfolk Hoy (2006) asked twelfth graders to nominate and evaluate teachers they felt helped them learn and become interested in studying a high school subject. The researchers interviewed top-scoring teachers and observed them teaching. They compared students' nominations to their class grades to verify that the students learned in the classes that their nominated teachers taught. The results of the study indicated that highly effective teachers show enthusiasm for the subject they teach, consider the subject important, show excitement, and show that they care about their students.

"High school students whose friends are low academic achievers tend to become less motivated to succeed in school and, over time, to prefer alternate activities that match their peers' beliefs." Unfortunately, this is true. The good news is that the opposite is also true: when students talk with friends inside and outside of school about ways to approach and improve their achievement, their motivation and self-regulated learning strategies increase (Jones, Estell, & Alexander, 2008).

Do adolescent children's abilities to play instruments and sing affect their self-esteem more than their ability to read music does? The answer is more complicated than true or false (a typical research finding!). Researchers Scalas, Marsch, Vispoel, Morin, and Wen (2016) found that children's rating of the importance of music reading varied widely. However, whenever children rated music reading as having high importance, children's self-esteem was more strongly related to their music reading ability than to their performing abilities (low self-concept when they perceived themselves to be poor readers and high self-concept when they perceived themselves to be strong readers). When children rated music reading as having low importance, their abilities to sing or play instruments were the only significant contributors to their musical self-concept.

Finally, "parents' expectations for and valuing of their children's musical studies are key to children's success or failure." Yes—that is true! Parents are critical to children's success in all areas of education, and especially in the study of music because of the high demands that music study creates for families' resources, attitudes, and support (McPherson, 2009). Before children enter a music classroom for the first time, they have impressions from their parents of attitudes toward music, their potential abilities to perform music, music's importance in relation to other subjects, and music's social value, among other things. Parents' approaches to their children's practice and musical study at home impact children's musical motivation, interest, progress, frustration, and achievement.

APPLICATIONS OF EDUCATIONAL PSYCHOLOGY

Teachers need to read, understand, and use educational research to improve their effectiveness and increase students' learning. Teachers also do research formally and informally in their classes. For example, you may be aware of your high school teachers' use of student learning objectives (SLOs), and recall taking pretests and posttests that measured your progress on those SLOs. In many states, teachers must determine SLOs for their courses based on state or national standards (see Chapter 10) and school district policies. In any course, an SLO should be the most important learning students should achieve in the course of their year of study.

Using research practices, teachers either design valid and reliable tests to measure students' learning, or they adopt other tests that measure them. For example, some school districts in New York State use solo or ensemble ratings forms from the New York State School Music Association (NYSSMA) to measure their students' progress toward performance SLOs in ensemble classes, like band, orchestra, and choir. To measure students' SLO achievement, teachers administer a test at the beginning of the year, *before* students begin work on the learning objectives. This initial test, known as a pretest, measures students' entry-level knowledge of the SLO. For example, some students may take piano, voice, or instrumental lessons outside of school in which they learn to read music and to perform at more advanced levels than their peers who do not study music outside of school. Teachers use pretest scores to determine students' initial knowledge and to compare that initial knowledge measurement with students' test scores at the end of the course on a posttest. The test designation of "pre" or "post" refers to the instruction that happens between administrations of the test. A pretest is given pre-, or before, instruction, or before students undergo the various learning activities and experiences the teacher guides them through in order to learn the SLO. A posttest is given post-, or after, students complete the activities and experiences designed to enable them to learn the SLO. Students' posttest scores indicate their progress toward accomplishing the SLO since their pretest scores at the beginning of the course. In states where teachers must set and test SLOs using pre- and posttests, administrators consider these measurements of students' progress in their evaluation of teachers' effectiveness.

Teachers also use educational research procedures more informally when they use evidence-based procedures to make decisions about their teaching. Imagine that you attended a workshop to learn how to use a music teaching approach in your general music classes. You are excited about this new approach, but you do not know whether or not it will help your students sing more accurately. You could

Fig. 5.2: Teachers need to read, understand, and use educational research to improve their effectiveness and increase students' learning.

plan and carry out action research in which you pretest the singing accuracy of students in two different fourth-grade classes you teach every week. After students complete the pretest, you compare the classes to determine whether or not their singing accuracy is similar. Because you choose two fourth-grade classes, you already know that the students' ages are comparable, and both classes had similar music lessons with you when they were in third grade. You decide to teach one of the fourth-grade classes using your usual teaching methods, and the other using the new approach you learned at the workshop. You teach both classes as well as you can, making sure to teach both in the same singing range, with the same songs, but with different approaches (e.g., perhaps different warm-ups, different tune-up patterns, different ways of breaking the songs down and putting them back together). You type informal notes into a document at least once a week, in which you record your impressions of students' reactions to the teaching methods, their attitudes about the new or the old approaches, and how you feel about teaching each way. After two grading periods, you again test the students' singing accuracy using a post-test. You sit down with your favorite beverage and look carefully through the students' singing accuracy scores to determine whether there are significant differences in their achievement. You review your notes to see how you felt things were going in week two, week five, and so on. After you consider both the quantitative data (the test scores) and the qualitative data (your journal), you might decide to interview some of the students to see how they thought their singing progressed. You consider all of these data—your evidence—and you make the best possible choices for the students you teach, based on what the evidence shows you about their learning.

As we have seen in the chapter on the history of music education and in the chapter on why you want to be a music teacher, schools directly reflect the society in which we live. Everything that happens to children at home and in the community has an impact on them and therefore on their ability to learn and understand information. When children are unable to feel safe at home, they will find it difficult to learn as easily as other children who do not have that burden of feeling unsafe.

ABRAHAM MASLOW

Abraham Maslow (1908–1970) was an American psychologist best known for his theory of the hierarchy of needs, which he originally proposed in 1943. His original model included five levels of needs

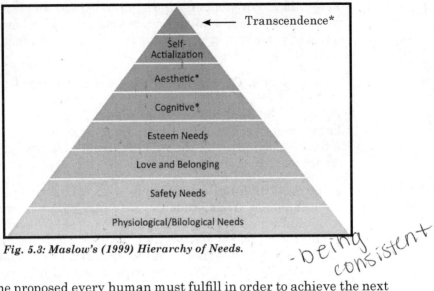

Fig. 5.3: Maslow's (1999) Hierarchy of Needs.

-being consistent

that he proposed every human must fulfill in order to achieve the next level. In the 1960s and 1970s, three more levels were added (Maslow, 1999). Figure 5.3 is a diagram of Maslow's Hierarchy of Needs. An asterisk is added next to the levels that were not part of the original five.

The important thing to remember with this hierarchy is that the bottom three needs (physiological/biological, safety, and love and belonging) are called *deficiency needs*. One cannot move ahead to the upper levels until the deficiency needs are met. The upper levels are referred to as *being needs*. In contrast to the deficiency needs, being needs are never fully satisfied. One desires more and more of each being need. For example, a person cannot learn effectively until he or she feels safe, fed, clothed, and so forth. Once the person meets those needs, however, he or she will have a desire to continue learning throughout life. The individual will not meet the need to learn once and move on.

DEFICIENCY NEEDS (1-3)

1. **Physiological and biological needs:** This includes shelter, food, water, sleep, and so on ... the things necessary to sustain life. In the classroom, this means that students who do not have enough food at home, those who do not get enough sleep, and homeless students will all have different educational

needs than will students whose physiological and biological needs are met. Students will not be concerned with how many quarter notes are in a whole note when they cannot know when their next meal will come.

2. **Safety needs:** Once children have what they need to live, they need to feel safe. This means they need to know that rules will be applied consistently and fairly. They need to know their teachers care about them and have their best interest in mind at all times. They cannot learn when they do not feel safe.

3. **Love and belonging:** Humans seek relationships with other humans. Your students, just like you, will want to fit in and relate to friends and family in their life who care about them. Social issues play a major part not only in the lives of your students, but also in students' classroom behavior. Friends talking to each other, children bullying former friends, students arguing over whom they like and don't like—these social interactions may seem silly to adults, but remember that they are important to your students, and therefore you must accept them and expect to account for your students' social interactions when you are planning and teaching.

BEING NEEDS (4–8)

4. **Esteem needs:** Self-esteem development is an important part of the maturing process. Great teachers provide many opportunities for student success and achievement in their classrooms. Giving specific and honest feedback helps develop self-esteem. Giving generic and vague feedback—such as simply saying, "Good!"—does not. Students need to see improvement in their knowledge and skills. Once they do, their self-esteem will improve. Setting up students to succeed musically and personally, and noticing your students as individuals, are ways in which teachers can make a big difference in this area.

5. **Cognitive needs** were added around 20 years after Maslow's initial hierarchy was published. Cognitive needs address one's need for knowledge. For music teachers, this is the

content knowledge your students can learn once they have met the previous four needs. Notice that this is the *fifth* need. Students can concentrate on their cognitive needs only *after* the needs lower in the hierarchy are met, yet cognitive needs are what teachers want to get to the most.

6. **Aesthetic needs** were also added to Maslow's hierarchy later; they concern a person's need for opportunities to appreciate beauty. Look back at the previous five needs, consider the possibility that you did not have those needs met yet—would you be willing or capable of appreciating something beautiful?

7. **Self-actualization:** Maslow proposed that only 1% of the population ever reach this level. This involves a higher level of thinking and refers to personal growth, reaching your full potential, and having a sense of fulfillment. It is likely that you will not be teaching students at this level, but you personally should think about your ability to meet this particular need.

8. **Transcendence** was also added later and refers to the topmost level, which involves helping others achieve self-actualization.

How does this relate to your becoming an excellent teacher? Part of it is to realize that while the topic of music is extremely important to you, it may not be to your students when they are dealing with a stressful home life and things like poverty and abuse. You need to make your classroom a safe environment where all students feel like they belong and take into consideration what might be happening to these children when they are not in school.

On a very minor level, you probably know what it feels like to not get enough sleep and then try to concentrate, work, or even drive. I have seen students falling asleep in classes, or valiantly trying to stay awake. They are clearly not getting as much from that class as they would be if they were sufficiently rested. How do you feel when you are hungry or thirsty? Can you concentrate on new information when your stomach is growling? When you are starting to get a headache from being so hungry? Now imagine if you were a child who is *always* hungry; who never has enough food or drink; who is only a child but is staying up late to take care of his or her little siblings. Perhaps that child is living in a shelter, or a car, or eats only one meal a day, if he or she is lucky. Clearly, the needs of that child are very different from those of a child who has the basic necessities. The disadvantaged child will obviously have a much more difficult time being an active participant in music class when those basic needs are not met.

CONCLUSION

When you use educational psychology in your career by reading research reports, gathering evidence of your students' learning, and reflecting on evidence to make instructional decisions, you will improve your teaching effectiveness and increase your students' learning.

REFERENCES

Arshava, I., & Kutepova-Bredun, V. (2015). The comparison of personal traits of the professional and amateur musicians. *European Scientific Journal, 11*(20), 46–55.

Box, C., Skoog, G., & Dabbs, J. M. (2015). A case study of teacher personal practice assessment theories and complexities of implementing formative assessment. *American Educational Research Journal, 52*(5), 956–983. doi: 10.3102/0002831215587754

Bruner, J. S. (1996). *The culture of education.* Cambridge, MA: Harvard University Press.

Centers for Disease Control and Prevention (CDC). (2015). *Trends in the prevalence of behaviors that contribute to violence on school property: National youth risk behavior survey (YRBS): 1991–2015.* Retrieved from https://www.cdc.gov/healthyyouth/data/yrbs/pdf/trends/2015_us_violenceschool_trend_yrbs.pdf

Jones, M. H., Estell, D. B., & Alexander, J. M. (2008). Friends, classmates, and self-regulated learning: Discussions with peers inside and outside the classroom. *Metacognition Learning, 3,* 1–15. doi: 10.1007/s11409-007-9007-8

Kemp, A. E. (1985). Psychological androgyny in musicians. *Bulletin of the Council for Research in Music Education, 85,* 102–108.

Lee, K., & Johnson, A. S. (2007). Child development in cultural contexts: Implications of cultural psychology for early childhood teacher education. *Early Childhood Education Journal, 35,* 233–243. doi 10.1007/s10643-007-0202-7

Li, J. (2003). U.S. and Chinese cultural beliefs about learning. *Journal of Educational Psychology, 95*(2), 258–267. doi: 10.1037/0022-0663.95.2.258

Long, J. F., and Woolfolk Hoy, A. (2006). Interested instructors: A composite portrait of individual differences and effectiveness. *Teaching and Teacher Education, 22*(3), 303–314.

Maslow, A. (1999). *Towards a psychology of being* (3rd ed.). New York, NY: John Wiley & Sons.

McPherson, G. (2009). The role of parents in children's musical development. *Psychology of Music, 37*(1), 91–110. doi: 10.1177/0305735607086049

Polit, D. F., & Falbo, T. (1987). Only children and personality development: A quantitative review. *Journal of Marriage and the Family, 49*(2), 309–325.

Scalas, L. F., Marsh, H. W., Vispoel, W., Morin, A. J. & Wen, Z. (2016). Music self-concept and self-esteem formation in adolescence: A comparison between individual and normative models of importance within a latent framework. *Psychology of Music,* 1–18. doi: 2443/10.1177/0305735616672317

Shaughnessy, M. F. (2004). An interview with Anita Woolfolk: The educational psychology of teacher efficacy. *Educational Psychology Review, 16*(2), 153–176. doi: 1040-726X/04/0600-0153/0

RECOMMENDED READING

Hupp, S., and Jewell, J. (2014). *Great myths of psychology: Great myths of child development.* Hoboken, NJ: Wiley-Blackwell.

DISCUSSION QUESTIONS

1. Your favorite teacher's or conductor's words, actions, and leadership likely affect your beliefs about good teaching, but these cherished memories can also lead to the trap of folk pedagogy. Identify and discuss with others a music teaching technique that, in your experience, was effective. Why do you think that technique worked for you? Can you imagine a setting or students for whom this technique might be *ineffective*?

2. Design a miniature study comparing practice techniques for accomplishing a performance goal, such as accurately playing rapid passages of notes or memorizing music. How could you measure and compare the success of the techniques? How could you be sure the effects of using one technique did not interfere with the effects of using the other?

3. Studies of teacher effectiveness indicate that calling on student volunteers to answer questions (folk pedagogy/tradition) is *less* effective in getting students to learn than using a system to call on students randomly (e.g., pulling students' names out of a hat, or rolling dice to determine what numbered student's name to call). What are some reasons why random calling of students' names could increase student learning?

4. Form a group of at least six classmates, in which more than one gender is represented. Make an informal seating chart indicating where everyone in the group sits in relation to one another during the experiment. One group member will take a turn as the teacher, ask a series of questions, and lead group discussion of a neutral topic, while another group member will tally on the seating chart how many questions were asked of each group member, and how many responses each group member made. Set a timer for five minutes. In that five minutes, the teacher will ask questions and lead discussion on this chapter, and the recorder will make notes on the seating chart. *Wait* until after you complete the five minutes of discussion to read the next part of this exercise.

After the five minutes end, all group members should examine the seating chart and discuss the data using these questions:

1. Did the teacher call on all students equally? (Unless your teacher used a system to ensure equal questioning, it is unlikely that the questions were distributed equally.)

2. Did students of one gender receive a greater proportion of questions than students of another? (In the United States, male *and* female teachers more frequently call on students who identify as male than on students who identify as female.)

3. Did the teacher call more frequently on students seated to the teacher's right or left? (Left-handed teachers tend to call more frequently on students on their left, and right-handed teachers tend to favor those on the right.)

4. Complete another five-minute discussion using a new seating chart and a different group member as teacher. However, this time you *know* educational psychology research findings 1, 2, and 3. Can you balance student questioning knowing these tendencies? (It's helpful to know the research, and it will take practice to put it to use in your teaching!)

5. When you are temporarily lacking in a specific need, (sleep, food, etc.), what areas of your life diminish? What do you find difficult to do when you need sleep or food?

6. What differences do you notice between the deficiency needs and the being needs? How many of the needs can you give examples for from your own life?

Image Credits

CHAPTER 6

CREATING LESSON PLANS

A lesson plan is exactly what it sounds like—a plan for the class that day. Schools, states, and educator preparation programs require teachers to write and maintain files of lesson and rehearsal plans. They need to include sufficient information in their plans to do the following:

a. Identify their students' learning needs, address those needs with experiences in classes and assignments, and assess students' learning to determine next steps.

b. Document the planning process, so that reviewers (professors, state certification test examiners, school administrators, etc.) who read the plans can evaluate and provide feedback on the teaching.

c. Provide legal records of the instruction students in classes and rehearsals have received.

There are many ways to write a lesson plan and many formats you could use. For the purpose of this book, I am going to stick to four main categories for creating a lesson plan:

1. **Objective:** This is what you expect your *students to learn and be able to do as a result of this lesson.*

2. **Standards:** These are state or national guidelines for what to teach students about music. Any standard you list in your plan must match the content of the objective in your plan. You

> If it is an *objective*, you have to assess it.
>
> An *objective* is what you are teaching *today*.
>
> An *objective* is specific
>
> *Procedure* is an outline of what you and your students will be doing during the lesson.
>
> An *assessment* can be anything that demonstrates your students' understanding of the content you are teaching.

must assess students' learning (or *not* learning) of any standards you put in your plan.

3. **Procedure:** This is a detailed outline of what you (the teacher) and your students will do, step by step, throughout the lesson.

4. **Assessment:** This is how you will know whether your students met (or did not meet) the objectives and the standards you said they were going to learn *that day*.

Every time you prepare to teach, you need to plan in each of these four categories. They are depicted in a cycle in Figure 6.1 because each plan component affects the next.

Objectives state what students will learn in the lesson, which links to national and state standards that list recommended goals for music learners. In order to teach students the objectives and standards of the lesson, you design procedures, which are the activities, rehearsal strategies, demonstrations, explanations,

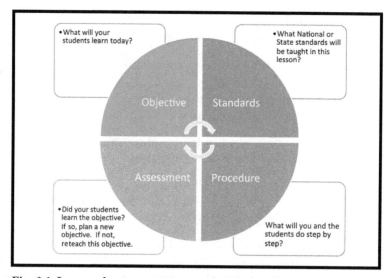

Fig. 6.1: Lesson plan components are interrelated!

questions, and exercises—the things you and the students will do during the lesson so that they can learn. You must plan assessments to do within the lesson to find out how well the students learned the objectives. The cycle continues after the lesson is over, because you use the assessment of students' learning today to decide what to plan for them tomorrow. Did students learn the objectives easily, making them ready to move on to different objectives, or do they need more instruction to learn today's objectives? Often students need some combination of the review of recent learning with introduction of new objectives.

OBJECTIVES

What, specifically, will your students learn *today*? What, specifically, will you teach your students *today*? It is *not* an objective to say that your students will play a piece of music today. Instead, teach students to play a piece of music because it will enable them to reach objectives involved in performing that music. For example, your students learn certain intervals contained within the piece of music, or they could discover and understand a specific musical idea, form, style, or technique that they will apply in that music. Your objective could be that students learn a specific rhythm pattern in the piece. Your objective could even be that students will improve their intonation in challenging parts of the music, or that they will adjust their performances to better balance melody and accompaniment.

Objectives that are vague fail to provide a record of students' learning that can be measured or proven. "Students will perform the notes and rhythms correctly" is an example of an objective that is too vague. This unspecific music objective is like a math lesson objective that states, "Students will do all math problems correctly today." The lack of specificity causes you to wonder, what *kind* of problems did they do? Addition? Multiplication? Calculus? Did the problems involve mathematical processes that were new to students or familiar to them?

Here is another example of the problems that vague objectives can cause. Let's say I told you to stand at a street intersection in downtown Manhattan, and I said that you could leave when you saw the sign. I did not explain to you what the sign would be, because it was something I assume would be obvious to you. Suddenly, as you are standing alone in busy Manhattan, waiting for the sign so that you can leave, you think, *The light turned green—maybe that's the sign? There is a car honking—maybe that's the sign? Here comes an adorable dog—that must be the sign!* However, it is impossible for you to know whether even obvious signs (green lights, car horns) are the sign for you to leave, because you do not know what you were to accomplish by standing on this corner or what sign would tell you that you had done whatever you were supposed to have done by being there in the first place.

To put this Manhattan intersection example back into the context of teaching music: Because you did not know the *objective* you were to accomplish at the intersection, you could not know what kind of sign would indicate that you met the objective, so you had no way to *assess* whether or not you met the objective and could leave.

When you plan lessons, you need to write clear and specific objectives for your students' learning so that you know when your students meet them (or when your students do *not* understand and need more or different lessons to learn the objectives). Here are some examples of specific and measurable objectives. Remember that objectives state what students learn and can do *because of learning* during lesson activity and instruction:

- Students will be able to recognize, chant, and perform eighth- and sixteenth-note rhythm patterns in 2/4 time using rhythm syllables.

- Students will alter their pitches using embouchure, positioning, and instrument adjustment to match model pitches in isolation and in musical context.

- Students will sing and match the vowels "ah" and "uh" with open throat and relaxed jaw in isolation and in lyrics, such as "father" and "water," in musical context.

- Students will be able to improvise 2-measure duple meter responses on rhythm instruments to 2-measure duple meter calls.

It is wise to limit your plans to one or two objectives because you must *assess every objective* your lesson plan says that students will learn that day. Your lesson procedures may plan many activities, demonstrations, practice sessions, and so forth that support students who are learning the objectives, but *unless you assess whether or not students learned* something, those activities themselves are not an objective. Conversely, if you set an objective for students to learn something, you must assess that something because you said it was the objective of the lesson.

STANDARDS

In 2014, the National Coalition for Core Arts Standards (NCCAS) developed a new set of core arts standards for dance, media arts, music, theater, and visual arts (State Education Agency Directors of Arts Education). The NCCAS is not a government agency, but rather a partnership of organizations and states that includes the National Association for Music Education, The College Board, and the State Education Agency for Directors of Arts Education, as well as similar organizations representing theater, dance, and visual arts. They are intended to help organize arts curricula by describing what every student should learn and be able to do as a result of arts classes in their Pre-K–12 schooling.

As you read the standards, remember that they describe what *students* will be able to do. Imagine each one beginning with the common phrase *"Students will be able to ..."*

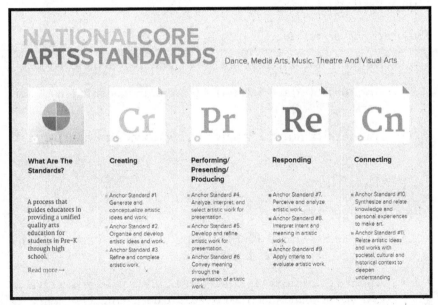

Fig. 6.2: National Core Arts Standards.

Creating

[Students will be able to ...]

- **Anchor Standard 1:** Generate and conceptualize artistic ideas and work.

- **Anchor Standard 2:** Organize and develop artistic ideas and work.

- **Anchor Standard 3:** Refine and complete artistic work.

Performing

[Students will be able to ...]

- **Anchor Standard 4:** Analyze, interpret, and select artistic work for presentation.

- **Anchor Standard 5:** Develop and refine artistic work for presentation.

- **Anchor Standard 6:** Convey meaning through the presentation of artistic work.

Responding

[Students will be able to ...]

- **Anchor Standard 7:** Perceive and analyze artistic work.

- **Anchor Standard 8:** Interpret intent and meaning in artistic work.

- **Anchor Standard 9:** Apply criteria to evaluate artistic work.

Connecting

[Students will be able to ...]

- **Anchor Standard 10:** Synthesize and relate knowledge and personal experiences to make art.

- **Anchor Standard 11:** Relate artistic ideas and works with societal, cultural and historical context to deepen understanding.

See more at http://www.nationalartsstandards.org/#sthash.IEzXtimi.dpuf.

The actual National Core Arts Standards document is quite involved. Go to the website, http://www.nationalartsstandards.org, and use the prompts provided there to view a detailed standards handbook for one of these music learning settings:

- Music classes, Pre-K–8

- Harmonizing musical instruments

- Music composition and theory

- Traditional and emerging ensembles

- Music technology

You can also choose from four different grade levels:

- Pre-K–2

- 3–5

- 6–8

- High school

As you can see, by using these choices, you are able to customize the standards on this website so that you can see the standards for exactly the age level and the class or ensemble you teach.

Implications Standards Have for Your Planning

Look through your lesson plans and ideas for plans—do you expect to teach certain standards and ignore others? According to the standards accepted by the membership of our national association, and to the title of "music" given to most states' teaching licenses, every music teacher's job is to be a well-rounded *music* teacher, not to be only a classical music teacher, or an instrumental music teacher, or a vocal music teacher, or a singing-songs music teacher. You are to be students' *music* teacher. As such, you should choose to work as much as possible on any musical area you do not feel comfortable

Fig. 6.3: To be the music teacher, you need breadth in musical knowledge.

teaching during your time in college (and afterward) so that you can feel confident teaching *music* to your future students.

Are you uncomfortable with improvisation? Join an improvisation group or take an improvisation class. Are you an instrumentalist who does not know how to play all the main instruments? Take as many secondary instrument classes as you can, get lessons, or trade instrument lessons with a friend who needs to learn your instrument. Do whatever you need to do to strengthen your knowledge in your weakest musical areas. Are you a vocalist who does not know much about instruments or who cannot yet accompany a choir on piano? Get help, get lessons, practice, and improve your skills. Be proactive about getting yourself ready to teach all the National Core Arts Standards. As you advocate for your own personal growth as a teacher, you will be advocating for the musical growth and education of your future music students.

PROCEDURE

The procedures in your lesson plan are an outline of what you and your students are going to do during the lesson. Procedures should be detailed enough for a substitute teacher to be able to use them to teach your lesson in your absence. Procedures should answer these questions: What are you going to do first? How are students going to get the materials they need? When? How are you going to introduce the topic? What questions will you ask students? What will they do to learn the objectives during the lesson? What are you going to do next? After that? How are you going to conclude the lesson and help students remember what they learned?

Education students in my classes also write in their plans what they will do when something *unexpected* happens. For example, if you write in your plan procedure that you are going to ask students what the word *forte* means, add to your procedures what you will do if your students do *not* answer that question correctly. It may seem that in a good lesson, students would answer all questions correctly, but, in fact, they should *not*. When students get all the answers in a lesson correct, that usually means they already know the content you think you are teaching them. If students know all the answers, why are you teaching that content? They already know it—so adjust your objectives and move on to teach what your students *need to learn*.

It is a good idea to think through how you are going to ask a question or give a direction, but avoid the mistake of reading from your procedures when you actually teach the lessons you plan. Before you get in front of students, practice your lessons enough that you know what is coming next, so that you avoid taking time to read from your lesson plan when you are teaching.

ASSESSMENT

As you write the assessments for your lesson, keep asking yourself this question: How do I know whether or not my students understand what I am teaching them? Assessment is not just looking around the room to get a general idea of whether or not most of your students can do the objective. You need to plan assessments that will enable you to find out, specifically, who in your class can do the objective and who cannot. You should be able to look back at your notes and your grade book a day or weeks after a lesson and see who learned the content, who could "do" the objective, and then use that information to inform your planning for the next lesson or unit.

For example, imagine that your lesson's objective is for your kindergarteners to correctly match your pitch. To assess this, you are going to sing a phrase to the children, and they will echo/respond to sing it back to you. To assess things effectively, you would need a checklist of some kind to mark down who was able to sing the phrase correctly, who was able to do it with prompting or help, and who could not do it (or would not attempt it). Imagine that you taught the lesson, and out of 24 students, 15 students could sing the phrase correctly the first time, 5 students could do it the second time when you reminded them to use their singing voice, and 4 students could not do it at all. From these results, I might conclude that my students are ready to move on to the next skill, but I need to include in my lessons going forward help for my four students who cannot yet match pitch. I must not ignore the fact that four students cannot yet match pitch just because everyone else could. I take the assessment results (i.e., that four students failed), and that information informs my next lesson, where I might try a different strategy to help those four individuals, include a warmup that helps them use their voice to explore different pitches and ranges, and so on as part of the procedures that also would address the objective in the next lesson.

Assessment has several key roles in lesson planning:

- Measures *students'* learning

- Matches learning that is defined in the objectives

- Informs your planning for the next lesson

- Addresses every objective in every plan

- Accurately measures whether or not students learned the objective. (For example, if your objective is for students to match pitches while singing, giving them a written test in which they listen to you sing two patterns and circle whether they were the same or different does *not* accurately measure the objective, because you assessed the children's ability to listen and recognize pitch patterns, not to match pitches while singing. To accurately assess the objective, you would need to instead have the children sing back to you the pitches you model.)

We will discuss assessment in greater detail in the next chapter.

REFERENCE

State Education Agency Directors of Arts Education. (2014). *National coalition for core arts standards*. Retrieved from http://www.nationalartsstandards.org

DISCUSSION QUESTIONS

1. Do you think you learned all the National Core Arts Standards equally during your elementary and secondary education? What, if any, standards do you think were weaker or missing from your education?

2. Give an example of a summative and a formative assessment you have experienced in a music setting.

3. Think of five ways to give specific praise to a student and five ways of providing constructive criticism.

4. Consider the most recent instrument or voice lesson you had. What do you think the objective of that lesson was, and how did your teacher assess whether you learned it or not?

5. What creative ways can you think of to assess students' music learning without using written tests or worksheets?

Credits

- Fig. 6.2: Copyright © 2014 by National Coalition for Core Arts Standards. Reprinted with permission.

- Fig. 6.3: Copyright © by Shutterstock Images LLC/Zarya Maxim Alexandrovich.

CHAPTER 7

ASSESSMENT

As we discussed in the lesson planning chapter, *assessment* is how you know whether or not your students learned the objectives of the lesson. You must assess every objective in any lesson plan, and, conversely, in order for something to be an objective, it must be assessed. In other words, implied in the definition of *objective* as "something toward which effort is directed: an aim, goal, or end of action" ("Objective," n.d.) is determining whether or not students *have met* the objective—the aim, goal, or end of action. What good is setting an objective if you never find out whether or not it was reached?

Try to remember a time in your student life when you were in a class in which the teacher taught something that, on that day, you could *not* learn. You left the lesson thinking, *I did* not *understand that*. Perhaps you could not learn it because you did not have enough previous knowledge about the topic to move to the next step the teacher thought you would be able to get to that day. Maybe the way the new information was explained did not make sense to you. Perhaps you needed to see more examples of a new process, you needed more explanation, or you needed guided practice to understand it. Do you remember whether or not the teacher seemed to know that you did not understand? How would the teacher have known? Assessment! The assessment that day might have been asking you if you had any questions, then listening carefully to find out which part of the objective did not make sense to you. Assessment can be in the form of quizzes, tests, or graded assignments, or it can be done by observing students' attempts to complete the objective during lesson time. All teachers assess their students' learning, most traditionally through written tests. However, the most effective teachers use assessments of their students' learning (and *lack of learning*) to direct their planning of the next day's lesson, and the next, and the next.

At the 2011 meeting of the Third International Symposium on Assessment in Music Education, experts in music education assessment from all over the world met to attempt to define what "effective music assessment" means. They came to agreement, and published their expert understanding of effective assessment (Bebauer, Winter, Schurig, & Campos, 2013, p. 247) as

- A process of collecting information/data, and

- Making a judgment, often in relation to a standard or an expectation

- With the claim to improve, and

- That results in improved and continued learning and/or teaching.

DIAGNOSTIC, FORMATIVE, AND SUMMATIVE ASSESSMENTS

There are three different kinds of assessment:

1. **Diagnostic assessments** are used to pretest or find out what students already know and what they still need to learn. Diagnostic assessments enable you to determine the baseline knowledge and skills that each of your students has related to the objectives the class will be learning.

2. **Formative assessments** are used to improve or enhance new performance skills, knowledge, or actions that are *not* graded (assessments done while students' knowledge is *forming* to

Key Words for Assessment	
Feedback	Summative
Formative	Diagnostic
Reliability	Validity
Norm-referenced	
Criterion-referenced	

enable both the students and the teacher to determine the students' progress, gaps in understanding, need for re-explanation, etc.). For example, when a teacher gives students feedback during a rehearsal or class, that feedback is formative assessment, because it tells students how they are doing while they are in the process of learning the objective. Formative assessment helps students learn the objective by validating their correct attempts and redirecting, reviewing, or teaching differently after students' incorrect attempts.

Teachers' feedback is so important for students' learning! Instead of responding to students' efforts with an indefinite "Good job," effective teachers offer formative assessment that says what, exactly, students did well or what they could do to improve. If a small group of students performed everything perfectly (which is rare!), for example, other students in the class could learn from a teacher's formative assessment response of, "Wow! You performed that rhythm perfectly, and you kept a steady beat. Well done!" In addition to praising students' efforts, this specific praise would tell everyone else in the room that  the rhythm they just witnessed performed with steady beat was the target for their performance.

Students who do not understand an objective benefit from formative feedback that enables them to understand that their performance is not yet correct and what they need to do to improve. Often new teachers have the idea that telling students "Good!" all the time will encourage them and help their self-esteem. In fact, the opposite can be true.

For example, in an elementary classroom, if I sing a pattern of two pitches for children to match, and they sing a different pitch pattern back to me, telling them "Good!" is not encouraging; it's teaching them *incorrect* information. The pitches the children sang were *not* the same pitches I modeled. Although the children's effort might have been good, or they might even have sung more accurately than the last time they tried, the actual pitches they sang were incorrect. In this case, "Good!" from the teacher could actually teach students that their incorrect response was correct because it praises inaccurate singing.

Instead of automatically saying, "Good," effective teachers give their students specific feedback to help them learn. For example, "Your pitch was lower than mine. Here's the pitch you sang [sing their pitch], now try singing my pitch [sing new pitch]." If the new pitch is still inaccurate, instead of saying, "Good!" be more specific: "You did sing a little higher that time; you are moving in the right direction! Next time, we will work on singing the exact pitch I sing." Given this response, students can understand that although they improved, they still have work to do, and they know exactly what they need to improve (moving their voice pitch higher).

Educational consultants Jackie Acree Walsh and Beth Dankert Sattes (2005, p. 89) report six research-based ways to respond to students who give incorrect answers or responses when called upon. I added musical examples in brackets [ ] after each of Walsh and Sattes's strategies.

- **Cue:** Use symbols, words, or phrases to help student recall.

   [If a child sings pitches that are below your modeled pitches, use the symbol of sliding your hand in the air from a lower level as you sing the child's pitch to a higher level as you vocally glide your voice from the student's response to the correct starting pitch. Signal the child to place a hand forward and attempt to match your vocal glide to feel and hear the voice rising.]

- **Clue:** Use overt reminders, such as "Starts with ..."

   [If a child cannot recall the fingering for the note indicated, give clues, such as, "You know the F-sharp is here, and this is F-natural. Which is higher or lower? How do you play a tone lower than F-sharp?"]

- **Probe:** Look for reasoning behind an incorrect response or ask for clarity when the response is incomplete.

   ["You are right that we say someone has an accent when their way of speaking sounds different to our ears. How do you make your notes sound different to our ears when they have accent markings on them?" In this case, the teacher uses the child's reasoning of what an accent is to help the child grasp the meaning of accents in music.]

- **Rephrase:** Ask the same question in different words.

[Your first question ("Was your pitch in tune with hers?") receives a vague or an incorrect response. Rephrase the question: "Did your pitch and hers sound smooth together, like one sound?"]

- **Redirect:** Pose the same question to a different student.

[Use this option when a student is unable to answer, even after you offer a supporting cue, clue, probe, or rephrase.]

- **Hold accountable later:** Later in the lesson, check back with the student who responded incorrectly to make sure that the student can now answer correctly.

[In addition to ensuring that the mistaken student now understands, returning to mistaken students to check for understanding teaches everyone in the class that your purpose in giving feedback is to support students' learning, *not* to reward and punish by sorting students into "good musician/bad musician" or "talented/untalented" groups.]

3. **Summative assessments** are used to grade students' performance at the completion of a lesson or unit (in summary). Summative assessments include ranking students (e.g., seating according to playing ability in an ensemble), or assigning a number or letter grade for a project or for learning completed within an entire semester. Summative assessments can take the form of anything that measures students' learning—from written tests and worksheets to projects, presentations, performances, or group work.

When planning any assessment, you need to think about what you are really assessing. For example, if I were to give you a written exam on this chapter, in addition to assessing your knowledge of the chapter, I would also be assessing your ability to do things that have little to do with your understanding of the chapter, such as your ability to read the test, to write, to follow directions, to remain quiet and seated, to focus your attention, to answer questions within a specific amount of time, and so on. For this test to be a valid measurement of your knowledge, I would need to take steps to reduce the possibility that these collateral aspects of written assessment could interfere with your ability to show your true subject knowledge on the test. For example, I would need to check the difficulty of the vocabulary and reading complexity of the test to make sure it was age- and reading level–appropriate. I would review the test's directions and ask others to read and explain them to me so that I could improve their clarity. I would practice taking the test and compare its content with other tests I have given students at your level to accurately estimate how much time you would need to comfortably answer all the questions. When planning an assessment, you need to consider and minimize the effects of things an assessment measures that have nothing to do with the test's objectives, because these collateral aspects of assessment can influence the results and interfere with the test's accuracy and fairness.

Once again, giving specific and accurate feedback to students on their performance on summative assessments is critical to their learning. You must give your students more than just a letter or number grade, so that they can learn and grow from the experience. For example, imagine that you turned in a paper assigned for this class, and I handed it back to you with the comment "Poor! D–." You would know from the grade that your paper did not measure up to my expectations, but you would not know what exactly to do differently the next time you wrote a paper for the class. How would you interpret my insistence that your work was "poor" in combination with the information that you very nearly failed the assignment? Because you received no specific criticism, explanation of your paper in relation to the objectives of the assignment, or instructions for attempting improvement, you would have no feedback you could apply to increase your learning. *What* did you do poorly? Was your choice of topic wrong? Was your grammar inaccurate? Did you make wrong conclusions? Was your paper too short? Too long?

You would have more opportunity to learn if the paper that I handed back to you contained constructive feedback that explained what aspects of the assignment were below standards. Students face the same inability to improve when their assignments are marked simply "B+." What did you miss that kept this work from earning an A? What did you do well enough to earn a grade better than a C?

RELIABILITY AND VALIDITY

If you open any textbook about assessment, you likely will find definitions and explanations of reliability and validity within the first chapter because they are the fundamental characteristics of objective assessment.

Reliability: An assessment is reliable when it consistently yields the same score, regardless of the scorer. A yardstick or a meter stick is a reliable tool for assessing length, because once one understands how to use it correctly, the measurement it yields will be the same no matter who uses it or how many times one measures something with it.

> **Example 1:** Mrs. Isabella gives a multiple-choice exam wherein students identify which instruments are playing after listening to recorded examples. The test answer choices are either right or wrong, so no matter who grades the test with the answer key, the test score will be consistent. Therefore, the test is reliable.

> **Example 2:** Mrs. Isabella has each member of her orchestra play a solo so that she can judge the quality of the students' playing ability. She grades their solos with standard letter grades (A, B, C, etc.). Another music teacher who heard Mrs. Isabella's students might judge their playing to be quite poor, because that teacher's expectations of sound quality, technique, and so on differ from Mrs. Isabella's expectations. Yet another teacher might listen for each player's improvement and judge the solo performances more favorably than Mrs. Isabella did. Because Mrs. Isabella's letter grade assessment has no specific criteria that different judges can use to assess consistently, it is unreliable. A rubric that defines playing ability by listing criteria and various achievement levels within each criterion would be a more reliable assessment than undefined letter grades, because it would yield more consistent scores.

Validity: An assessment is valid when it measures what it intends to measure. (This is more difficult to accomplish than it may seem.)

> **Example 1:** Mrs. Richner gives a written test to see if her class has learned how to play the flute. The test consists of a fingering chart in which students color in the holes they would cover to produce various notes they have learned.

Mrs. Richner's fingering chart test is an invalid assessment because it does not measure what she intended to measure, which is whether or not her students can *play* the flute. Instead, the test measures whether students can correctly complete a fingering chart.

Example 2: Mrs. Richner wants to assess her students' ability to match pitches by singing. She has students echo her singing two pitches in a pattern individually and in pairs, and she scores their pitch matching using a rubric that awards four points for matching within a half-step, three points for matching within a third, two for matching within a fifth, and one for matching intervals wider than a fifth from the pattern she modeled. This assessment is valid because it measures students' ability to match pitches by singing, which is what Mrs. Richner intended to assess. Having students sing in pairs as well as individually mitigates the issue of performance anxiety students might experience when singing alone.

An assessment cannot be valid if it is not reliable. Why? We defined *validity* as measuring what one intends to measure. If your assessment tool is unreliable, it will yield different results, even when you use it to measure the same thing over and over. Because you cannot obtain consistent results from an unreliable assessment, you cannot be certain it is a valid measurement of what you intend to assess.

ASSESSING MUSICAL PERFORMANCES

One of the greatest assessment challenges music teachers face is the need to assess students' live performances in valid and reliable ways that provide students with the feedback they need to learn and to progress as music makers. When students perform, whether improvising, chanting solfège, playing their compositions, or performing solo or ensemble parts, they literally *make music*. It is invalid to assess students' music-*making* skills by asking them to complete a written test on the key signatures, composers, or historical contexts of the music they performed, or even by asking them to critique a recording of their performance. When you assess students' critiques of performances, you assess their ability to respond to, analyze, and evaluate performances—all valuable aspects of musicianship—but assessing critiquing skills fails to assess students' musical *performing* abilities.

Teachers often use rubrics, which consist of grids that contain specific performance criteria and defined levels of achievement for each criterion (see Figure 7.2), to assess students' performances and other kinds of class work. Rubrics enable teachers to translate performance assessments into numbers they can use to include students' performances in music course grades, explain students' progress to parents and administrators, and help students use feedback to improve their performance. Students can participate in making appropriate rubrics to assess their own performances. Whether or not you involve students in creating rubrics, it is essential that students have copies of and understand the rubrics you will use to assess their work. Encourage students to use the clear guidelines that rubrics provide to set goals that can improve their performance.

Rubric for Instrument Lessons

	1	2	3	4
Notes	Few notes played correctly.	More notes played correctly than incorrectly.	All but a few notes played correctly.	Notes played correctly throughout.
Tone	Sounds unsupported.	Sounds supported when prompted.	Sounds supported on long notes.	Sounds consistently supported.
Rhythm	Few rhythms played correctly.	More rhythms played correctly than incorrectly.	All but a few rhythms played correctly.	Rhythms played correctly throughout.
Expression	Played same dynamic throughout.	Played marked dynamics one or two times.	Played all but a few marked dynamics.	Played marked dynamics throughout.

Fig. 7.1: Example of a rubric for elementary wind or brass instrument lessons.

Limit the rubrics you design to three to five levels (Brophy, 2000) to avoid overwhelming students with information while still providing enough guidelines for consistent scoring. The strategies listed below are among those recommended by music education assessment expert Darrel Walters (2010, pp. 82–83), based on his experiences in educating teachers about assessment:

- **Limit rubric/rating scale criteria to a single dimension.** Whenever you use the word "and" in a rubric, you tie together performance aspects that students may do separately. For example, if you write, "Rhythm and pitches performed accurately," the student can achieve this level only by performing the combination as described. How would you score a performance in which the pitches were performed well but the rhythms were less accurate?

- **Use positive language.** Write rubrics that count what students did instead of what they left out. You can better assess something that is present than something that is missing.

- **Be realistic.** Your rubric should set goals that your students can attain. Avoid using words like "perfect," "absolute," or "optimal." You should also avoid describing completely unacceptable performances ("terrible," "abysmal," "awful"). Rubric levels award points, so even a single point earned should correspond to a valued performance aspect the student demonstrated.

- **Use precise language.** State what the desired attribute is, avoiding subjective words like "good," "poor," or "average," and vague numbers like "sometimes" or "often."

CRITERION- AND NORM-REFERENCED ASSESSMENTS

You are beginning to understand the different reasons for assessment, the importance of reliability and validity in assessment, and ways to assess performances with greater reliability. When you assess students' knowledge, performance, or skills, you must also determine how to interpret their scores. What does it mean if a student earns a score of 16? Does that score indicate mastery of the exam, as it might if that were the student's score on the rubric in Figure 7.2? Does that score indicate competence? It might if it were the minimum number of correct answers on the written test taken to earn a driver's permit. Where did the student's score of 16 fall among the scores of all other students in the state who took the same exam? Was 16 the top score, in the middle of the scores, or at the bottom? Tests can be interpreted in reference to established criteria, like understanding the rules of for driving in your state, or in reference to the typical perfor-

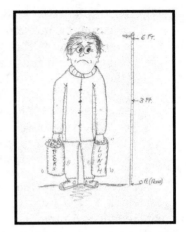

Fig. 7.2: In criterion-referenced assessment, students are compared to an established standard or target.

mance of people who take the exam, like the national "norms" for college entrance exams.

Criterion-referenced: Compares all students' scores to the same standard.

> **Example:** Ms. McKay gives students a composition assignment. In order to receive an A, a student must compose eight measures in common time using four different rhythms and at least six different pitches. For every note or criteria students fail to follow, they lose a point. Using this criteria, every student in Ms. McKay's class could earn an A. This composition assignment is criterion-referenced, because students' performance on the assignment will be evaluated against established standards.

Norm-referenced: Compares students' scores with each other or to typical, normal scores.

Fig. 7.3: In norm-referenced assessment, students are compared to each other.

Example: Ms. McKay gives the same composition assignment, but this time she grades it based on how everyone in the class did. She reviews all the students' compositions, and then determines which is the *best* in the room. The best composition earns an A. The composition that is the *worst* in the class earns the lowest score. A composition that is better than the worst one, but not as good as the best one, gets a grade in the middle. She interprets each student's accomplishments in relation to the results from the entire class.

Before you decide that Ms. McKay must be a terrible teacher, consider that this kind of norm-referenced sorting is exactly how music teachers commonly interpret auditions: "You are the best, so you sit here; you are not quite as good, so you sit there." If you instead seated an ensemble based on a criterion-referenced test, you would give students a set of criteria they could meet in order to be first chair (which would result in multiple "first chairs"). If you were ever in a class in which the teacher graded your tests "on a curve," you experienced norm-referenced grading. If the highest test score in that class was a 70, that score earned an A, and the remaining test scores earned grades respectively below that.

ALTERNATIVE ASSESSMENTS

Although you will sometimes need to use written assessments in music teaching, remember that there are many other creative and engaging ways to assess whether or not students learned the objectives. These are just a few of the many options:

- Games
- Projects
- Portfolios
- Performances
- Blogs
- Skits/plays

- Compositions
- Cartoons
- Journals
- Podcasts
- Radio broadcasts
- Original dances

Assessments inform you, the teacher, what your students are learning and enable you to decide what next steps to take so that they can make progress. Did the students learn the material? If so, move on; if not, review, focus on the specific things the assessment showed students were unable to do, and teach the material again, perhaps differently. You can assess learning effectively using many ways—performance assessment, written assessment, and numerous alternate assessments—for students to demonstrate their understanding.

REFERENCES

Bebauer, H., Winter, C., Schurig, M., & Campos, S. (2013). The culture of shared practice: Key issues for assessment in music education work session summary. In T. Brophy & A. Lehmann-Wermser (Eds.), *Music assessment across cultures and continents: The culture of shared practice.* Chicago, IL: GIA Publications.

Brophy, T. S. (2000). *Assessing the developing child musician: Guide for general music teachers.* Chicago, IL: GIA Publications.

Objective. (n.d.). *Merriam-Webster.com.* Retrieved February 5, 2017, from https://www.merriam-webster.com/dictionary/objective

Walsh, J. A., & Sattes, B. D. (2005). *Quality questioning: Research-based practice to engage every learner.* Thousand Oaks, CA: Corwin Press.

Walters, D. (2010). *A concise guide to assessing skill and knowledge with music achievement as a model.* Chicago, IL: GIA Publications.

DISCUSSION QUESTIONS

1. Review the definition of *effective assessment* published by the experts who attended the Third International Symposium on Assessment in Music Education. Which parts of this definition do you think make assessment an effective teaching tool? What are the reasons for your answer?

2. Imagine it is your first day as a student teacher in a large suburban high school that has several ensembles in your area of expertise (band, orchestra, or choir). You learn from your supervising teacher that you will spend your first hour of student teaching leading a sectional for students who are in an ensemble. What kind of diagnostic assessments could you

do early in the lesson to find out what these students need to learn to make progress?

3. Why is it imperative that you assess every objective in any lesson you teach?

4. Students in Mrs. Innes' music classes have been learning to imitate, chant, read, and improvise rhythms in duple meter using eighth notes and quarter notes and rests. Would a written test in which students wrote the counts for various duple rhythms be a valid test of the students' rhythm learning? Why or why not?

5. What are three benefits students gain from formative feedback? How does formative feedback help teachers?

6. Mr. Smith is writing a rubric he can use to assess his students' rap improvisations. He decides that the first criterion will be rhythmic stability or "keepin' da beat." Using Walters's (2010) strategies, suggest levels of achievement students could aim for when keeping the beat in their raps.

Rappin' Rubric			
1	2	3	4
Keepin' da beat			

7. Aside from driver's license tests, what other criterion-referenced tests have you taken? How do you know that your example was a criterion-referenced test?

Image Credits

- Photo by Laura M. Dornberger.

- Fig. 7.2: Copyright © 2016 by Thomas Dornberger. Reprinted with permission.

- Fig. 7.3: Copyright © 2016 by Thomas Dornberger. Reprinted with permission.

CHAPTER 8

TEACHING ALL STUDENTS

For me, the real joy of teaching music has always been that music is something almost everyone can relate to in some way or another. Almost everyone likes *some kind* of music. Not everyone loves math or reading, but nearly everyone has some connection to music. You may enjoy music most by being a wonderful performer, and someone else may be a great listener, but music has an important role for both of you.

This chapter will briefly explore the wide variety of students you will encounter during your music teaching career. The broad term for variety in learners is *special needs*. Special needs includes any students who have unique needs that teachers must consider so that these students can learn as effectively as everyone else.

STUDENTS WITH DISABILITIES

In 1975, Congress enacted the Education of All Handicapped Children Act (Public Law 94-142) to ensure, for the first time in the United States, that children with disabilities had the opportunity to a free and appropriate public education, just as nondisabled children had. In 1970, just a few years before Public Law 94-142, U.S. schools educated only one in five children with disabilities, and many states had laws that excluded disabled students from public schooling (U.S. Department of Education, 2007). In 1997, the law was amended significantly, and its name changed to the Individuals with Disabilities Education Act (IDEA).

With many amendments and updates in the decades since then, IDEA remains the United States of America's federal special education law. In the most recent update of IDEA (2006, §300.8), Part 300 specifically outlines 14 different categories of disabilities for classification and protection for accommodations by federal law. When a school's committee for special education (CSE) meets to discuss a student's educational needs, that child's disabilities are classified under one or more of these 14 categories, and therefore the school must make accommodations, by law, in order for the student to be provided with the educational opportunity to learn as well as nondisabled peers can. Special needs accommodations *do not* give students an advantage—they simply allow students who have disabilities to have what they need in order to have a fair chance to learn.

Consider this: Imagine that I walk into a classroom where 5 out of 20 students are wearing prescription glasses. Would it make sense for me to tell the five students wearing glasses to remove their glasses because they have an unfair advantage to the other students in the class?

Does wearing glasses mean they have superhero eyesight that puts them unfairly ahead of the class? Of course not. Wearing glasses is what they need to do in order to see as well as everyone else. Special needs accommodations for children with disabilities are the same thing—they provide learners with disabilities what they need in order to have the same opportunities as nondisabled learners.

It is also important to note that although we categorize disabilities and mention strategies that can help learners whose needs fall into these categories, learners are *children*, and therefore no one is exactly the same as anyone else, even when they have disabilities classified in the same categories. The *child* should be your focus, not the disability.

When speaking or writing about children with disabilities, it is important to remember that children are children *first*, and they happen to have disabilities. So, instead of saying, "There is an autistic child in my choir," we say, "A *child* with autism is in my choir." Word order may seem like a small matter, but it means a lot when you remember at all times that the child is the important one, not the disability. When disabilities interfere with a child's learning, you change the instrument, the music, the lesson, the assessment, the objective, the method, the procedure, and so on to make learning possible. You do *not* change the child.

According to IDEA Part B (2015), schools must create an individualized education program (IEP) for each student identified as having one or more disabilities that interfere with his or her ability to learn. Students' IEPs are written and managed by a committee that considers information about the students' diagnosed disabilities, reports from teachers and specialists, parents, and state and federal laws, and sets in place a plan for what accommodations each student needs in order to have a fair chance at learning. Accommodations may include things like time-and-a-half for testing (e.g., if the rest of the students get an hour to finish the test, the student with this IEP would get an hour and half to complete the test), reduced choices for testing (e.g., if you give a multiple-choice test and give everyone four choices, the student with this IEP may get three choices per question), and needing to have lecture notes written for the student.

Whatever accommodations are listed in the IEP are *mandated* for implementation in every lesson in the student's schedule, including music classes and rehearsals. As a teacher of students with disabilities, you have the responsibility to read and follow the directives the IEPs of all students in your classes. Teachers who choose *not* to follow IEPs can face legal consequences. The accommodations listed in IEPs are there with good reason, set by professional educators who have specific knowledge of the student's diagnoses, needs, and sensitivities, as well as the student's parents/guardians, to give the student the opportunity to be successful in your class.

Below, I have quoted the 14 definitions of disabilities that are listed in the Individuals with Disabilities Education Act [§300.8 (b) concerning developmental delays and definitions (c) (1)-(13)]. According to IDEA, these definitions apply to education for children ages 3 through 21. Keep in mind that in order to receive special education services, a child's educational performance must be adversely affected by at least one of the listed disabilities. In other words, if children have medical diagnoses of a disability listed below, but that disability does *not* have an impact on their ability to learn, they are not eligible to receive special education services.

After each definition, I offer suggestions of teaching approaches that may help accommodate students with these disabilities in music classes. I also include a list of sources for further reading at the end of this chapter to help you continue your learning in this important and complex area of teaching and learning.

1. **Autism:** A developmental disability significantly affecting verbal and nonverbal communication and social interaction, generally evident before age three, that adversely affects a child's educational performance. Other characteristics often associated with autism are engagement in repetitive activities and stereotyped movements, resistance to environmental change or change in daily routines, and unusual responses to sensory experiences. The term *autism* does not apply if the child's educational performance is adversely affected primarily because the child has an emotional disturbance as defined in definition 4 below. A student who shows the characteristics of autism after age three could be diagnosed as having autism if the criteria above are satisfied.

The most effective ways to help any child with a disability are to be informed, to know the child, and to teach in ways that will not only help the child with a disability, but all the other students in the room as well. Children with autism may be resistant to coming to your music room because it is different from other classrooms, they are not as familiar with the surroundings, and they may be very uncomfortable with all the sounds that will be prevalent in your room.

Tips for teaching students with autism (note that every one of these tips are excellent for everyone in the room, but crucial for the child with special needs):

- Make the directions you give in class very clear—write them, show them, and speak them. Children with autism are unable to pick up on subtle social cues like facial expressions and sarcasm. They need accurate, clear directions.

- Give the child a schedule for the day's class, and try to maintain specific routines for everyone as they enter and leave the classroom, take out and put away instruments, and so on.

- Have a plan with students with autism so they know what to do if they are feeling overwhelmed. For example, they may

Excerpts from: U.S. Department of Education, from "Sec. 300.8 Child with a Disability," IDEA Regulations, Part B. 2004.

be allowed to go into a quieter and darker area, such as an adjoining practice room, to reduce sensory overload.

- Work with the child and his or her parents/guardians so that you know what works best for the child and what he or she needs from you. The child may need music that is not too loud or jarring, visuals that are clear but not too busy, or visual reminders in the room of where to go or what to do if he or she needs to self-soothe or calm down.

2. **Deafness:** A hearing impairment so severe that a child is impaired in processing linguistic information through hearing, with or without amplification, which adversely affects a child's educational performance.

When you are planning for a student who is deaf, you need to make sure that your visuals are clear and contain the information the student will need to be successful during your lesson—not only in the content area of music, but also in directions, procedures, rules, and safety issues.

Tips:

- Directions and expectations need to be written and posted so that every student can refer to them throughout the lesson.

- Use your skills as a conductor! *Show* your students what you want them to do instead of telling them. Do you want the class to stand up? Indicate it with a gesture rather than by telling them. *Leading by gesture not only helps your student who is deaf learn; it is also excellent to teach all your students to watch the conductor for meaningful instruction.*

- Make sure you have instruments such as low drums, so that the student can feel vibrations and the beat.

- Do not seat children with a hearing impairment next to you when sitting in a circle. They need to be able to see your lips moving.

- Face the student at all times when speaking, and make sure your mouth is visible, not covered with your hands or obscured by a curtain of long hair.

- Use gestures and pointing for clarification when giving verbal directions.

- Consider using items/videos that show the sound waves and vibrations from different pitches.

3. **Deaf-blindness:** Concomitant [simultaneous] hearing and visual impairments, the combination of which causes such severe communication and other developmental and educational needs that they cannot be accommodated in special education programs solely for children with deafness or children with blindness.

A child who is profoundly deaf and blind would probably not be placed in music classes. However, children who participate in music may well have both hearing and visual impairments. It is important to remember that these children cannot see facial expressions or hear tone well enough to respond normally, so it is important to make directions and expectations clear in other accessible ways. All crucial directions and expectations need to be spoken *and* written, using gestures and pointing to help clarify.

- Make sure you remove tripping hazards from your room and notify support staff of the times when the student is in your room each week. You will need help to get that child to safety in an emergency, so it is important that everyone knows that child's location throughout the school day.

- Talk with the child and his or her parents, aides, special education teachers, and other teachers to determine what works best for that child.

4. **Emotional disturbance:** A condition exhibiting one or more of the following characteristics over a long period of time and to a marked degree that adversely affects a child's educational performance:

   a. An inability to learn that cannot be explained by intellectual, sensory, or health factors.

   b. An inability to build or maintain satisfactory interpersonal relationships with peers and teachers.

   c. Inappropriate types of behavior or feelings under normal circumstances.

   d. A generally pervasive mood of unhappiness or depression.

   e. A tendency to develop physical symptoms or fears associated with personal or school problems.

The term also includes schizophrenia. The term does not apply to students who are socially maladjusted, unless it is determined that they have an emotional disturbance.

To work with any student with special needs, you need to make sure that you speak with the student's support system—the special education department, the student's family, and other teachers to understand what works and what does not work in helping this student reach educational goals.

- Make sure you and the student establish a plan for what the student should do when he or she is feeling overwhelmed, angry, upset, and so on. This plan can include self-soothing techniques, having the child remove himself or herself to a safe space in the room, or having the child go to a separate room in the building that has been designated as safe and appropriate. Your options for the student's relief depend on the age of the child and the system already in place at your school. Whatever you both decide will work best needs to be used consistently. The procedure and/or place should be something the child can self-assign and that you can assign as well.

- You need to watch all students at all times for signs they are understanding, bored, off-task, and so on, but it is crucially important to keep your eye on children with emotional disturbance. Knowing particular students' signs of growing stress and making sure you intervene *before* an incident occurs are very important. Teachers who learn to notice warning signs can intervene before a student's growing anger and frustration escalate to an incident of acting out that derails learning and that can be dangerous to the student with emotional disturbance and other students in the class (Colvin, 1993).

- Interventions that help deescalate acting out can be as simple as breaking down the instructions for an assignment or a rehearsal segment into smaller manageable steps, or getting the student to attempt to begin work and supporting that attempt (an important sign of willingness to learn) with praise and brief directions for taking the next step (IRIS Center, 2005a, 2005b).

- Have very clear rules, directions, and expectations for the entire class and be consistent in implementing them. Again, this is very important for all students, but crucial for a child with emotional disturbance.

5. **Hearing impairment:** An impairment in hearing, whether permanent or fluctuating, that adversely affects a child's educational performance but is not included under the definition of "deafness."

Many new teachers make the mistake of having a student who has a hearing impairment stand or sit next to them. Students who are hearing impaired need to sit in such a way as to be able to see the teacher talk so that the child can read lips if he or she is able. Do not assume that you can speak loudly throughout the lesson—you will not remain consistent. Make sure your student can see you and that you clearly print and post all directions and explanations somewhere the child can easily see.

Tips (the first two are the same for deafness):

• Are you giving verbal directions? Make sure they are written as well.

• Use your skills as a conductor! *Show* your students what you want them to do instead of telling them. Do you want the class to stand up? Indicate it with a gesture rather than by telling them. *Leading by gesture not only helps your student who is deaf learn; it is also excellent to teach all your students to watch the conductor for meaningful instruction.*

• Allow children with hearing impairment to use headphones if it helps them, rather than listening to large speakers in the room.

• Use instruments for demonstration that the child can hear well. You may need to speak with the child or parent/guardian ahead of time to see what works best.

6. **Learning disability:** A disorder in one or more of the basic psychological processes involved in understanding or in using language, spoken or written, that may manifest itself in the imperfect ability to listen, think, speak, read, write, spell, or do mathematical calculations. The term includes such conditions as perceptual disabilities, brain injury, minimal brain dysfunction, dyslexia, and developmental aphasia. The term does not include learning problems that are primarily the result of visual, hearing, or motor disabilities; of an intellectual disability; of emotional disturbance; or of environmental, cultural or economic disadvantage.

Learning disabilities are the most common category of disabilities. A child with a learning disability will have an IEP that reflects the accommodations and modifications the child needs to be able to learn.

As indicated in the definition, learning disabilities do *not* result from intellectual disability. A child with a learning disability has normal or above-normal intelligence, but has a disorder that affects use of spoken or written language. Once again, it is essential that you read the student's IEP and consult the special education department and the child to determine what works best for that individual learner. Accommodations may include

- Extended test time

- Reduced choices on multiple-choice tests

- Having a test read to the student

- Simplified worksheets

- Modified objectives

- Letting the student know ahead of time that you will ask a specific question so that the child has time to process the question and the answer

- You may need to supply the student with notes or a visible organizer of new information to be covered before class.

7. **Intellectual disability:** Significantly subaverage general intellectual functioning, existing concurrently [at the same time] with deficits in adaptive behavior and manifested

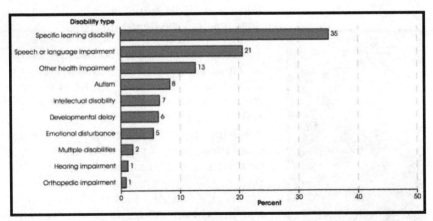

Fig. 8.1: Percentage distribution of children ages 3–21 served under the Individuals with Disabilities Education Act (IDEA), Part B, by disability type: School year 2013–14.

NOTE: Deaf-blindness, traumatic brain injury, and visual impairment are not shown because they each account for less than 0.5 percent of children served under IDEA. Due to categories not shown, detail does not sum to total. Although rounded numbers are displayed, the figures are based on unrounded estimates.

during the developmental period, that adversely affects a child's educational performance.

As always, you will need to speak with the special education department and the child's other teachers and consult the student's IEP to know exactly what is needed to help a child who has an intellectual disability. Some accommodations may include

- Alternate assessments: For example, perhaps this student would have tests read to him or her and would answer verbally instead of in written form.

- Alternate objectives: For example, the student may need to learn a different objective or fewer objectives than the rest of the class. The nondisabled students in the class may learn two or three objectives, while this student may only learn one per lesson.

- Extended time for testing, homework, classwork, etc.

- Additional supporting materials, such as open-book tests, a word bank, outlines of the class and material covered, etc.

8. **Multiple disabilities:** Concomitant [simultaneous] impairments (such as intellectual disability–blindness, intellectual disability–orthopedic impairment, etc.), the combination of which causes such severe educational needs that they cannot be accommodated in a special education program solely for one of the impairments. The term does not include deaf-blindness.

Fig. 8.2: Ensure inclusive learning environments that enable each learner to meet high standards.

This category is perhaps the most ambiguous because it includes all cases of students who have disabilities in more than one category. There are many potential combinations of disabilities, each resulting in unique sets of challenges. Sometimes it is appropriate to use the tips from more than one category, and sometimes it is more appropriate to use different strategies that work because of the individual student's challenges and abilities. The options for accommodating multiple disabilities completely depend on the needs of the child. Before you plan classes that include a child with multiple disabilities, you need to gain clear understanding of the child's IEP, because it will contain the most complete and accurate information you need to develop appropriate lessons and accommodations.

9. **Orthopedic impairment:** A severe orthopedic impairment that adversely affects a child's educational performance. The term includes impairments caused by congenital anomaly, impairments caused by disease (e.g., poliomyelitis, bone tuberculosis), and impairments from other causes (e.g., cerebral palsy, amputations, and fractures or burns that cause contractures).

The first thing to remember when accommodating orthopedic impairment is the rule that you change the instrument; you do *not* change the child. There are many adapted instruments you can purchase or make to help someone hold a mallet they otherwise could not grip or play an instrument when it seems that the person may not be able to. To make these accommodations, you have to think outside the normal playing procedures for instruments.

Story time: I was asked to help a student who had only one arm and who really wanted to play the cello. I ended up pairing her with another child who was a beginner. They both played the same cello, with one child doing the bowing, and the other child playing the fingerboard. They switched roles, depending on the piece they were playing. Both children experienced success and enjoyed playing the instrument. There are many stories such as these.

I know a professional saxophone player who suffered a stroke and lost the use of his right arm. He was able to get his saxophone customized so that he could play all notes with only his left hand. Now, this adapted instrument was very expensive, and his family and medical team applied for a grant to cover the cost, but the point remains that it *is* possible to change instruments to accommodate the needs of the player. Do not assume that a child cannot play an instrument because of his or her abilities or disabilities. There is almost always a way to make accommodations. On the other hand, you need to thoughtfully share with children and their parents the difficulties they may face trying to play a given instrument. If they ask your opinion, make sure you are honest with them and tell them the limitations of each instrument and also benefits of playing other instruments. In the end, it is incumbent upon you, the teacher, to listen to your students and find a way for them to play the instrument in which they have interest. Instead of thinking like a trained musician seeking perfect performance options and conditions, be a problem solver and see what you can do to facilitate your students' learning.

10. **Other health-impairment:** Having limited strength, vitality, or alertness, including a heightened alertness to environmental stimuli, that results in limited alertness with respect to the educational environment, which

   a. Is due to chronic or acute health problems such as asthma, attention deficit disorder or attention deficit hyperactivity disorder, diabetes, epilepsy, a heart condition, hemophilia, lead poisoning, leukemia, nephritis, rheumatic fever, sickle cell anemia, or Tourette syndrome; and

   b. Adversely affects a child's educational performance.

The category of "other health impairment," similar to "multiple disabilities," is a general category that could include a wide array of issues. Students with other health impairments will have special needs that vary widely, so, again, your best resources are the special education department, the IEP for the child, and the child's family. Whatever the child needs to be able to achieve the same (or modified) objectives is what you need to supply during your lesson. It could be something as simple as seating children in the front row to make it possible for them to see or leave quickly, allowing them to make up work, or letting them use a stress ball during the class. It could be something that would benefit everyone in the class. For example, adding movement throughout every lesson helps keep learners engaged, but it is especially effective for the child with ADHD (attention deficit hyperactivity disorder). You may need to excuse children with other health impairment from a movement activity because they lack the stamina or flexibility to do it, or because they easily get out of breath. If you know that a child will be unable to do a music class activity, find another way for that child to "play" with the musical material they need to learn or to have their learning of the musical material reinforced. Do *not* just let the child with special needs sit and watch everyone else moving, because that passive inactivity limits the child's ability to learn the musical material. If the movement activity was designed to reinforce or teach rhythm, for example, you need to come up with another way for that child who cannot do the movement activity to learn the same material.

11. **Speech or language impairment:** A communication disorder such as stuttering, impaired articulation, a language impairment, or a voice impairment, that adversely affects a child's educational performance.

As shown in Figure 8.1, speech or language impairment is the second most common category of disability. Of course, you know by now that I will start by saying that you need to consult with the special education department, the child, and the IEP to find out exactly what the child needs. In general, here are a few things to think about:

- When you plan to call on students to read aloud, you need to first find out if that is a good strategy for this student. If it is, make sure you are patient while the child reads, and you must quickly correct the class if they are impatient or disrespectful. If it is not considered a good idea to have that student read aloud, you need to be sure to avoid accidentally calling on the student to read, and you need to make sure you *do* call on the student to do something that does not involve speaking or reading (this could be "Show me how many ..." complimenting a movement, etc.)

- You need to be very clear in stating and enforcing rules and expected behavior. Bullying can be a big problem for any student, but it is an especially common problem for students with speech impairments. You must have zero tolerance for bullying, and the most effective way to deal with it is to stop it before it happens by maintaining a safe and organized classroom in which you can observe, teach, monitor, and enforce positive behavior.

- Speech impairment may (or may not) affect a child's ability to articulate when playing wind or brass instruments. It is common practice to invite children to try different instruments before choosing an instrument to study in order to determine which instruments they find comfortable and interesting. This is especially important for children with speech impairments. I have worked with many children whose speech impairments did not affect their performance until more advanced and uncommon articulation techniques, such as flutter tonguing, were introduced. Some students will be more successful and comfortable with an internal articulation source, such as a single or double reed. Others will find greater success playing brass instruments where they articulate using tongue and teeth, and the entire instrument is outside the mouth. Obviously, string and percussion instruments require no interaction with children's articulators; however, many students with speech impairment enjoy and succeed in playing wind and brass instruments.

12. **Traumatic brain injury:** An acquired injury to the brain caused by an external physical force, resulting in total or partial functional disability or psychosocial impairment, or both, that adversely affects a child's educational performance. The term applies to open or closed head injuries resulting in impairments in one or more areas, such as cognition; language; memory; attention; reasoning; abstract thinking; judgment; problem solving; sensory, perceptual, and motor abilities; psychosocial behavior; physical functions; information processing; and speech. The term does not apply to brain injuries that are congenital or degenerative, or to brain injuries induced by birth trauma.

Traumatic brain injury can result in many different challenges, depending on the child and, of course, the injury. A child with a brain injury could have physical limitations, behavioral problems, cognitive limitations, or any of the impairments listed in the category description. The IEP for that student will list the specific needs associated with helping that child learn. You need to be patient, kind, thoughtful, and clear when making plans and modifications for all students, but especially for students with traumatic brain injuries and other health impairments. Accommodations and modifications may combine strategies from other disabilities or recommend entirely new ones. In the end, it is crucial that you find a way to make sure that this child has the opportunity to learn from you.

13. **Visual impairment, including blindness:** An impairment in vision that, even with correction, adversely affects a child's educational performance. The term includes both partial sight and blindness.

Children with visual impairments will usually be able to tell you what they need from you. Do they need an enlarged copy of anything you put on the board? Do they need Braille versions of songs or handouts? For general accommodation, make sure you explain everything that goes on in class as it happens. Did someone just walk in the room? You can say, "Hi, Maya is here! Have a seat, Maya ... ." Information like this is very important to help students with visual impairment know that you include them as members of the class. Avoid using phrases like "Over there ...," "Watch me ...," and "Just like he is doing ... ." Instead, say specific things, like "Over there, on your right," "Watch me, I'm going to raise my right hand over my head," and "Just like Brennan, I want everyone to swing your arms back and forth to the beat." Comments like these give everyone in the room a clear indication of what to do, but they are crucial to the person who cannot see what is happening. Be a commentator throughout the lesson by saying what is happening.

Consider your assessment. Does this student need something different from you in order to fairly and accurately demonstrate understanding of the material? Do not expect that having the student sit in the front of the room will solve every vision problem and prevent you from having to make any other accommodations. Make sure you know exactly what that student needs to be able to fully participate in *every aspect* of the class.

Safety is very important! Make sure the paths in your classroom are clear of books, bags, instrument cases, carpet squares, and other tripping hazards. Do not rely on another student to take care of this student. It is not the responsibility of a child to take care of another child. Although other children may mean well and help when they can, their job is to learn music when they are in music class. Because they are immature, children can easily make a situation unsafe without meaning to do so. Children, their education, and their safety are your responsibility when they are in your class.

14. **Developmental delay:** For children from birth to age three (under IDEA Part C) and children from ages three through nine (under IDEA Part B), the term *developmental delay,* as defined by each state, means a delay in one or more of the following areas: physical development, cognitive development, communication, social or emotional development, or adaptive [behavioral] development.

As always, the first recommendation is that you talk to the special education department and review the IEP for the specific recommendations for the child. Make sure all your lessons are created with *every* child in mind and that you are meeting all the child's IEP recommendations at all times. In many cases, children with developmental delays will need extra support for learning. Some accommodations could be the following:

- Providing the student with a modified assignment. An example of this would be if you were handing out a worksheet with ten questions; this student may get a sheet with only five questions, to give the student more time to understand and process the questions. You should pass out the worksheets in a way that prevents the class and the student from knowing that there is a difference in worksheets.

- Making sure the student gets appropriate instrument choices to help him or her be successful. This is important when the student's developmental delays affect physical coordination and dexterity.

- Giving the student extra time to complete an assignment or assessment.

- Giving the student alternate assessments or assignments so that the child can be successful by demonstrating to you what he or she learned, just in a different way from nondisabled peers.

OTHER SPECIAL NEEDS

Many students have special learning needs that are not disabilities. One such need is English learning for students whose language of origin is *not* English, and therefore, who are learning to speak and read English at the same time they are studying other school subjects. Title VI is a federal law that prohibits schools (and other government funded entities) from discriminating on the basis of race, color, or national origin and requires school districts to take affirmative steps to ensure that English learners can participate meaningfully and equally in educational programs and services. Gifted students,

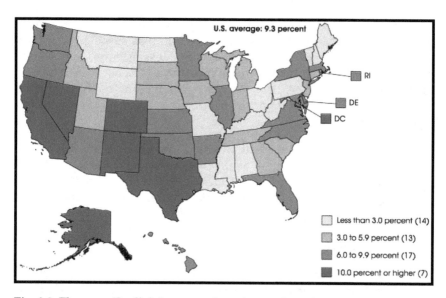

Fig. 8.3: There are English language learning students in every state.

sometimes called "gifted and talented" to broaden the definition of intelligence, are another group of learners who have special needs; however, there is no federal law that mandates special education for gifted students. Regulations concerning this group of learners varies by state.

ENGLISH LANGUAGE LEARNERS

As the shading on the map in Figure 8.3 indicates, there are English language learners (ELLs; students whose first language is not English) in every state, and the number of ELLs is rising. The first important thing to say about teaching ELLs is that students learning English do *not* have learning disabilities, and they should *not* be treated as if they do. Consider this: If you went to another country where the language spoken was one you did not know, and you sat down to learn in a classroom there, would your IQ be lower than it is when you learn in English? Would you suddenly be less intelligent than you are now? Of course not! You would still be the same person you are now, but you might certainly feel as if you were less intelligent because there would be so much information coming toward you that you did not understand. It is important to have empathy for ELL students. They have to work more than twice as hard at absolutely every task than everyone around them does. They need to remember what is being said (containing many unfamiliar words), think of it in their native language, translate it into English as best they can, and then act on the information.

Whenever people learning new languages need to learn in schools, they must deal with the words and conventions from two different language uses (IRIS Center, 2011). The first is basic interpersonal communication skills (BICS). This is the language people use on a daily basis—for example, "Hello, how are you?" "Where is the restaurant?" "Where is the bathroom?" Phrases like these are things a tourist would say, things you say among friends, and phrases for which you can easily find translations if you are looking at translation dictionaries or apps.

The second kind of language skill that children need to learn well in school is called cognitive academic language proficiency (CALP). Cognitive academic language is language that is used in academic settings. You might assume that English learners who can talk informally (i.e., use BICS) also know the words and expressions used in academic settings, but usually they do not. This is because people use academic words much less often than they use interpersonal communication. Academic language includes words like "compare," "list," "examine," "evaluate," "consider," and "contrast." When did you last hear words like those on television, in song lyrics, or while shopping at a mall? CALP also includes the words and discourse needed to study various academic subjects. In music, for example, we expect students to learn the terms we use to express dynamics, play various instruments, analyze musical form, read notation, perform with phrasing, recognize tempo markings, and so on. To learn in school, the English speaker needs to use words to construct higher-level meanings by inferring, considering implications, and using language for more complex functions than a tourist would ever use. Cognitive academic language is far more difficult to translate than interpersonal communication, and it takes English learners longer to achieve proficiency. The good news is that ELLs learn *both* BICS and CALP at the same time, but not at the same rate. Children's knowledge in their native language also affects the rate at which they learn CALP. For example, children who learned to make inferences in their native language need only to learn the translation of "infer" to know how to begin, but children for whom "infer" is a new and unfamiliar skill have no knowledge of what is expected of them in any language, and must learn the new process within the less familiar language.

• Tips for teaching ELLs effectively:

Label: If you have a student or students who speak a particular language and do not know many words in English, make sure you label everything in your classroom that you can. Put a sign on your stand with the word for "stand" in the students' native language and in English. Put signs on the piano, instruments, desks, light switch, door, board, books—anything to which you will refer when teaching. This is a simple way to not only include your ELL students, but also to help teach another language to all your native English speakers.

Visuals: Most of our daily communication is visual. The look on my face will tell you if I am kidding or if I am upset. We use hand gestures, eye contact, and so forth to communicate nonverbally. Remember that these kinds of nonverbal communication are crucial for ELLs. If I say, "Please stand up and go to the door," these students may not understand. However, if I say the same phrase while looking at them, indicating with my hands to stand up, and then point to the door, I greatly increase the chance that they will understand my direction.

Apps: There are several great translation apps that take written and spoken input and then play and show the translation. Although you will not want to rely on this for every conversation, you can use it when you have a particular problem explaining something, or to make sure that students can tell you about something they need. Literal translations are not always helpful, because there are so many different meanings for words when we use them in combinations, but basic translations may be enough to clarify a word or phrase. Also consider translating documents for not only the child, but their family as well. Information for school concerts and assignments needs to be available for everyone in the child's family to read. Do everything that you can to make the transition to speaking another language easier and more inclusive for your students.

Speaking: Have you ever heard someone speaking another language and thought about how quickly they were speaking? It always sounds fast when you do not understand it. When teaching classes that include ELL students, you need to remember to speak clearly and slow your speech *a little* so that you can be understood more easily. Do not shout or speak unnaturally, and remember to emphasize the important words just like you would normally. The ELL student will need to get context clues from the way you speak, so make sure you pause between sentences and pronounce all your words as clearly as possible.

GIFTED AND TALENTED STUDENTS

It may seem as if having gifted and talented students would make a teacher's life easier. In many cases, however, students who are gifted and talented can present some major classroom management issues. If you are a child, and you are always the first one done with tests, and you still get a perfect score, you are not being challenged or educated appropriately. As a teacher with gifted students, you can plan different objectives and assessments for your advanced students so that they are challenged to learn from your lesson as much as other students in the class. It is not appropriate to expect gifted students to sit quietly and wait while you teach the rest of the class. It is also not appropriate to have gifted students serve as teachers. Although they may learn some important things by teaching others or by helping struggling students, their job is not to teach; it is to learn. Gifted students are not grading assistants, even if they are willing to help you. Instead of putting them to work for you, you need to give them more challenging objectives to achieve. Defaulting to having advanced students tutor others denies them the education they deserve, even when they love teaching others and tell you they want to go into teaching. Find ways to provide teaching experience *in addition* to challenging their music learning. Like their peers, children who are gifted or talented are in school to learn, and you are the content expert who knows how to teach. Just as it is not right to ask a student to be in charge of helping a student with a visual impairment, it is inappropriate to ask a gifted child to act as a teacher instead of getting an education.

Consider teaching a composition lesson in which your objective is for the students to be able to write four measures in common time using skips and steps from middle C to the F line in treble clef with quarter, eighth, and half notes. Your objective for your advanced student could be to create a longer composition, perhaps with two parts, concentrating on phrasing, and adding accompaniment or lyrics, and so on. There are many ways you can teach the same main topic in class, but still have your advanced students engaged in learning throughout the lesson. Adjust your expectations for advanced students and plan for their learning experience, just as you do for everyone else in the room. If the gifted students are done first, what is the next logical step for them to learn? Where does that topic lead? It is important to remember that fair does not always mean equal. Students who are gifted may need to have more required of them because that is appropriate for their development. Do not have them waste learning time to draw a picture, grade your papers, or put their head down and wait for their peers. Use the time to teach them and enable them to learn and grow.

REFERENCES

Colvin, G. (1993). *Managing acting-out behavior*. Eugene, OR: Behavior Associates.

Individuals with Disabilities Education Act of 2004, 20 U.S.C. § 1400 (2015). Retrieved from https://legcounsel.house.gov/Comps/Individuals%20With%20Disabilities%20Education%20Act.pdf

The IRIS Center. (2005a). *Addressing disruptive and noncompliant behaviors (part 1): Understanding the acting-out cycle*. Retrieved from http://iris.peabody.vanderbilt.edu/module/bi1

The IRIS Center. (2005b). *Addressing disruptive and noncompliant behaviors (part 2): Behavioral interventions*. Retrieved from http://iris.peabody.vanderbilt.edu/module/bi2

The IRIS Center. (2011). *Teaching English language learners: Effective instructional practices.* Retrieved from http://iris. peabody.vanderbilt.edu/module/ell

U.S. Department of Education. (2007). *Archived: A 25 year history of the IDEA.* Retrieved from https://www2.ed.gov/policy/speced/leg/ idea/history.html

RECOMMENDED READING

Hammel, A. M., & Hourigan, R. M. (2011). *Teaching music to students with special needs: A label-free approach.* New York, NY: Oxford University Press.

Jellison, J. A. (2015). *Including everyone: Creating music classrooms where all children learn.* New York, NY: Oxford University Press.

Malley, S. M. (2014). *Students with disabilities and the Core Arts Standards: Guiding principles for teachers.* New York, NY: John F. Kennedy Center for the Performing Arts. Retrieved from http:// www.nationalartsstandards.org/sites/default/files/Guiding%20 Principles%20for%20Inclusion.pdf

DISCUSSION QUESTIONS

1. What accommodations have you seen teachers and students use in the music classroom? Did they seem effective to you? Why or why not?

2. Imagine that you have a student who comes to you wanting to play the trumpet, and that child has use of only her left arm. What could you do to make that happen?

3. A student with emotional disturbance is in your third-grade general music class. Unorganized time and loud noises trigger this student, causing him to be very upset. When he gets upset, he often hits himself and other children. What are three strategies you can use to help this child succeed in your classroom?

4. A child with a visual impairment is in your first-grade general music class. You are doing a lesson using lots of movement. What are three strategies you can implement to help this child be safe and participate in this learning activity?

5. A child with autism is in your choir. She gets upset when she is surprised and things are not predictable. List three strategies you can use to help this child succeed in your classroom.

6. Your high school band includes a child with a severe hearing impairment who plays in the percussion section. What are three strategies you can use so that this child can understand and learn the material?

Credits

CHAPTER 9

STRATEGIES FOR TEACHING

The journey from being a student to becoming a teacher is a long one. You have been a student all your life, so changing your perspective can be quite challenging. The main thing to remember as you become a teacher is that you will be the adult in the room. Let me repeat that: *the only adult in the room.* You will be responsible for the health, well-being, safety, education, and musicianship of hundreds of children. (Breathe ... keep breathing....) Teaching is quite an undertaking, and everything you do as a music education major in college is intended to prepare you for that challenge. From requiring you to dress, speak, and act professionally when you teach/present, to designing the classes you take, to giving you assignments to complete, the people preparing you to become a teacher hold you responsible and accountable for your behavior at the levels required of teachers. Teachers work with children whose rights and safety they must protect. You must learn to speak and act in a professional manner to enable your students to learn and grow in a safe and educationally sound environment.

Here are just a few specific tips that will help you in your progression toward becoming a professional teacher.

PROFESSIONAL SPEECH

The most important thing about professional speech is to think about what you are saying *before* you say it. You probably speak a little differently when you speak to a grandparent, versus a parent, a sibling, a friend, or a stranger. When speaking to these different people, you may use different vocabulary, different phrases, and different intonations. When you want to communicate with someone, you think about what words or attitudes you will use and words or attitudes you will *not* use, depending on to whom you are speaking. When you are speaking to students, you need to remember that you are not speaking to your friends. You must use a different way of speaking that is professional. Speaking professionally is not only about using better grammar and not swearing (although professionals do both those things!). To speak as a professional, you must think before you speak, and you must choose words and tone that are appropriate for your audience.

Over many years of educating teachers, I have found that requiring them to avoid saying "guys" is a great way to help them think about what they are saying before they say it. Consider this: "Guys" is what you call your friends. You say it without even thinking, as almost everyone does in America (and in other countries now, too) … and *that's* the problem. When you habitually say whatever comes out of your mouth without thinking about it first, you are far more likely to swear, use sarcasm, use hurtful criticism, and generally say things that are inappropriate, and therefore unprofessional, when speaking to children. Although it may seem harmless to call your students "guys" (despite the gender bias inherent in the word), you need to eliminate "guys" from your professional language to become mindful about what you say.

Instead of "guys" or "you guys," try saying "you," "everyone," "third graders," "friends" (to Pre-K through first graders), "students," "musicians." Using any of these words shows that you recognize your role as the adult in the room who is charged with children's learning and safety, and that you are thinking of your choice of words before you speak. Remember that "you" can be singular or plural, and it does not need a qualifier. "You" can refer to everyone in the room. The sentence, "You need to make that crescendo more gradual" is complete, and can refer to *all* the students in the ensemble. Pay attention to how often you and others say "guys," and when you are speaking in presentations and teaching, try to eliminate the word from your vocabulary. At first it will be very difficult to notice when you say it, but over time, you will find that you hear it as you say it, and then you will hear it in your mind right before you say it. When that happens, you will be on your way to being completely mindful about what you say before you say it.

GIVING DIRECTIONS

Most of you would agree that teachers should not ask their students directions; they should *give* their students directions. In reality, however, almost every teacher candidate asks directions instead of giving them, especially when first learning how to teach. Many new teachers say that they feel they are being mean to children when they give directions instead of asking for cooperation. They think it is nicer to ask children to do something, rather than to tell them what to do. Consider this—what is actually *mean* about stating clearly what your students need to do? When you ask students to do something, can they freely choose whether or not to do it without interfering in the lesson? For example, if you ask them, "Will you please stand up?" and they do not, is that alright with you? *Asking* students to do something gives them the impression that they have a choice. Whenever you would view children who are *not* doing what you asked as misbehaving, you likely asked them to do something when you should have *directed* them to do it. If you *ask* your class to do something, they should be able to honestly answer yes or no without being seen as uncooperative or misbehaving. Therefore, if you ask children if they want to sing a song again, and they all say no, move on. However, if you expect them to sing the song again either way, do not ask them; *lead* them ("Let's sing it again with more clarity in the second verse!"). Do not ask a question of children if you do not want an answer from them. Consider the examples below:

	Instead of ...	Try ...
1.	"Can you please stand up?"	"Please stand up!"
2.	"If you could come forward ..."	"Come forward ..."
3.	"We are going to sing this again, OK?"	"We are going to sing this again!"
4.	"We are going to start the project now, OK?"	"We are going to start the project now—does everyone understand what we are doing?"

Table 9.1: Ineffective Versus Effective Teacher Directions

Example 1: Do you really intend to give the class the option to stand or sit? This question does. Is there a reason you think the children cannot stand up? This question could imply you think so. Children are, by their nature, immature—immaturity is literally the definition of being a child. If you signal, by questioning, that the students have a choice, they may take advantage of that and choose to stay seated. If a student's choice to stay seated would annoy you or interfere with the lesson, you made a mistake when you asked students to stand instead of directing them to stand.

Example 2: Many new teachers start directions with "if." "If" is not the beginning of a directive sentence. "If you could come forward, that would be great" still gives students the impression that you are simply suggesting it would be nice, rather than directing them to do something.

Examples 3 and 4: Both of these examples begin with a direction but change it into a question with the addition of "OK?" at the end. The "OK?" tagline again signals to children that you are asking their permission to give that particular direction when, of course, you are not. Often "OK?" is filler, like "umm" or "uhhh," that has unintended consequences. You may insert "OK?" because you are trying to remain positive and encouraging, but asking "OK?" after a direction does not have that outcome. Instead, it implies to students that you have insecurity about this direction, and that you need their approval to move ahead.

The other instance of asking "OK?" after a direction happens when the teacher wants to see if the class understands. When this is the case, you have two options that are more effective than the confusing message "OK" sends. The first is to ask directly, "Do you understand?" or to ask for a signal (e.g., "Thumbs up if you understand ..."). The second way is to structure your lesson to give your students the opportunity to *show* you that they understand by, for example, moving correctly to their project stations *pianissimo* and putting materials in order to begin work. Students' correct or incorrect actions may offer you a more accurate assessment of their understanding than their nods that they do or do not understand directions.

ASSESSING THE MANY OR THE FEW?

As a teacher, you will constantly assess your students' learning. You will check to make sure they are paying attention, safe, behaving, understanding content, understanding directions, and so on throughout every lesson. One way teachers get feedback from their students is by asking them questions. Whom you ask, when you ask, and how you ask those questions can have a big impact on the accuracy of your assessments and your classroom management.

Many new teachers ask general questions to the entire class, instead of asking questions of particular children. Inexperienced teachers report that they do this because they do not want to single out a student who may not know the answer. But does it make sense to avoid finding out which students do not understand what they are trying to learn? Your job is to teach students information and skills they do not yet know! Therefore, wrong answers should not be avoided; they should be celebrated, because you find out who needs to learn and what it is that these students do not understand. The way in which you respond to wrong answers can create an atmosphere of learning and creativity in your classroom ... or it can create mistrust, anxiety, and inaccurate assessments. Consider the following:

	Instead of ...	Try ...
1.	"Who can tell me?"	"Noah, please tell me ..."
2.	"Can anyone tell me?"	"Show me on your hands how many ..."
3.	"Does anyone know ... ?"	"Barbara, what does this mean?"
4.	"Raise your hand if you can tell me ..."	"Everyone who thinks the answer is A, stand up."

Table 9.2: Ineffective Versus Effective Teacher Questions

In the first column, I give you examples of asking a general question to the entire class. This results in a few problems.

First, asking questions generally instead of specifically assesses only students who volunteer to give answers. Some of the students in classes where the questioning style in the first column is used may opt out of answering questions entirely. They can choose to do nothing and watch their peers answer, or their minds can be completely off task, not thinking about the lesson at all.

General questions send a message to the students who do not volunteer answers that the teacher only wants right answers, which can mean that wrong answers are bad and are to be avoided. Think about it—the question's wording asks "who can" or "can anyone tell me" the *right* answer. The unspoken accompanying statement is that the teacher does *not* want to hear any wrong answers. Sending students the message that you dislike hearing wrong answers creates a vicious cycle in which students who are unsure if they know the right answer avoid the risk of saying anything the teacher does *not* want to hear. These students may feel embarrassed, unwelcome, stupid, or—commonly in music classes—untalented. As time passes, they may become less and less likely to volunteer and participate in class because, in their minds, the repetition of this cycle proves that they do not belong. Children ascribe different reasoning to not belonging, such as, "I don't like that teacher," "That teacher does not like me,"

"I just don't like music," or "That class is dumb," or "boring," or "for losers," and so forth.

For the teacher, receiving answers only from the volunteering students who understand the lesson gives a false sense of the class's understanding of the lesson. Students who volunteer, usually know, or believe they know, the answers. Those who do not know the answers, or who think they do not know, often sit idly and watch, daydream, or misbehave instead of attempting to learn. Teachers cannot know what non-volunteering students understand about the lesson because they never check.

Calling for volunteers also sends students the (probably unintentional) message that the only students who matter in the class are those who choose to raise their hands. It sends this message because the teacher gives attention only to those who volunteer and leaves out those who do not. Adding impact to the teacher's hidden and explicit messages about volunteering answers is the fact that children are naturally immature, which means they can and will make poor choices. Because of their immaturity, they may choose not to direct their attention and effort toward learning. Children are also naturally egocentric, so they may assume in many situations that they are the root or cause of any problem. Therefore, instead of thinking, "Hey! I do not understand, so I'd better raise my hand and ask for help," they may think, "I am not very good at music because I do not understand this." Children should not have the choice to opt out of their own education, nor should they learn less than others because they are too immature to volunteer or to participate in class when the teacher did not seek their involvement.

General questioning often has a negative effect on class management. In all but one of the examples in the first column, the general question may lead to students' "shout-outs," or yelling out the answer without raising their hands or following any previously set rule. In many cases, teachers *accept* a shout-out when it is the *right* answer, but *correct* shout-outs when the answer is *incorrect* or unexpected. Think about the impact that inconsistency may have on students. Being consistent and clear about rules and expectations is crucial to creating an environment of safety and trust for students. What message are you sending your class when you get mad at them for shouting out wrong answers, but you are pleased when they shout out correct ones?

Avoid seeing wrong answers as a bad thing—wrong answers are *gold* to educators! Wrong answers let teachers know what and how their students are thinking. Because teachers know the material they are teaching so well, they often cannot remember what it was like *not* to know the material they are teaching. When you really understand something, it can be hard to imagine not understanding it. When all students have the opportunity to tell you what they think, you get great insight into what they understand and, if they do not understand, how they are thinking about it incorrectly.

> **Story time:** I once helped a friend of mine when her five-year-old daughter's piano teacher was out of town. My friend asked me to help her daughter, Sofia, practice her piano pieces for the following week's lesson. Sofia asked me where she should start, and I told her to start at the beginning. She started to play, and I saw she was not playing what was written. I stopped her and asked her which note she was playing, and she correctly identified the note she was playing, but that was not what was written. After further questioning, I had her point to what she was playing, and she pointed to the center of the music—the tenth measure of the piece. After seeing her confident response, I realized that Sofia thought that wherever she started was called "the beginning" because she was beginning there—a moveable point determined by her. Brilliant! Why wouldn't the place where you begin be called the beginning? I had known what "start at the beginning" meant for decades. I had not considered that it could be misinterpreted. If I had not encouraged Sofia to explain to and show me what she was thinking, I would not have known. I would have tried to correct a problem she did not have, which in

this case would have been correcting her note reading because I assumed she was misreading when, actually, she was reading correctly from a different part of the music. Sofia's wrong answer was crucial to enable me to understand what she was thinking.

NAME FIRST, THEN QUESTION

Most, if not all of us have probably experienced a teacher calling on a student in a "gotcha" circumstance. For example, the teacher asks a question, then calls on a student with a tone that clearly indicates the teacher believes that student was not listening. What is the purpose of this action? What does the teacher want to happen? In this case, the teacher is clearly letting the entire class know that the student called on was not paying attention. Oddly, the teacher in this situation actually wants the student to be *unable* to answer the question. If the student answers correctly, the teacher looks foolish, and the student demonstrates the ability to multitask, pay attention when appearing uninterested, and so on. If the student answers incorrectly, the teacher expects the student to be shamed, embarrassed, and supposedly "put in their place." The idea behind this teacher's action is that the student will listen more carefully to avoid future shame and embarrassment.

However, when you attempt to shame students by calling on them, you teach them that they cannot trust you, and that you will humiliate them when they make mistakes. When the purpose of questioning is to bring students' attention back to class and facilitate their learning, first say the student's name (in a professional and positive tone), and *after* you have the student's attention, ask the question. If the student, now given the chance to hear the question fully, is unable to answer correctly, provide help by breaking down the question or starting with the student's knowledge level and building to the original question, as teachers should do with every student. Given this different scenario, students will understand that the teacher observed that they were not paying attention, but that the teacher expects even off-task students to learn. This procedure can build trust by setting expectations, enabling positive learning experiences, limiting embarrassment, avoiding undermining student efforts, and avoiding starting a confrontational relationship in which the student begins to expect negativity and possibly challenges the teacher's actions.

FEEDBACK

Feedback is crucially important for teachers to do well. Saying, "good!" or "nice job" is useless feedback because it does not teach students anything, and it does not give them any information they can use to improve. To be effective, feedback needs to be three things:

1. **Accurate:** This seems obvious, but often does not happen. A teacher stops the ensemble during rehearsal (the group sounded awful), and the teacher says, "Good ... let's go back and try that again." Hearing this, the students in the ensemble think, "Um ... what was good about it? Why are we trying it again? Am I to play/sing exactly like I did the first time? Should I change something? What? Did the conductor hear how bad we sounded?"

   Most of the time, the feedback "good" is just a placeholder you say out loud while you are thinking about what went wrong, and trying to diagnose and fix problems. Perhaps you cannot think quickly enough about how to begin to enable students to improve such a poor performance, but that does not mean you should give inaccurate and unhelpful feedback.

2. **Specific:** "Good" does not tell your students anything meaningful because it is vague. Conversely, "Wow, that was terrible!" is also too vague to be useful feedback. *What* was good? *What* was terrible? If the performance really was good, was it perfect? Probably not, so what part do you want your students to do again, and what parts should they change?

3. **Content-related:** Your feedback needs to relate to what you want learners to learn/be able to do better. You may give students behavior-related feedback throughout a rehearsal or a class (e.g., "Sit up straight," "Eyes and ears on me"), but make sure you also give feedback that enables your students to get better at the music learning objectives you set for them.

After you give meaningful feedback, give your students an opportunity to work with it to fix the problem and then try again. Students need specific information and the opportunity to use it to improve their skill or understand the content better during that particular lesson. What do you do after students try to correct problems by using teacher feedback? You guessed it—you give more feedback (e.g., "Yes!

That's it!" or "Try one more time with this fingering instead of that one.")

Taking all of this into account:

	Instead of ...	Try ...
1.	"Good! Let's take it from measure 7."	"You played the rhythm in measures 1 through 8 correctly, but your intonation is not good. Let's sing through measure 7 and 8 to get that accidental."
2.	"Good! Let's do that again."	"I don't know what went wrong, but something did—let's try it again, and we will all listen carefully to see what it is."
3.	"Good job."	"That was great—you all got that key change and the rhythm that time. Let's do it again just like that, so that you remember it!"
4.	"Nice! Let's move on to another piece."	"Rhythm and pitches are inaccurate, but we are out of time—we will work on it next time."
5.	"That was terrible. Do it again."	"We clearly have a long way to go on this piece. We are starting at measure 12. Pay close attention to the key signature and watch me so that you know when to come in."
6.	"Close ..."	"You played the rhythm correctly, but you did not play together. Watch carefully and listen to synchronize."
7.	"No. Who can help this person?"	You are the teacher—you are the one who can help the student. Work with the student to arrive at the correct answer. If needed, offer answer choices.

Table 9.3: Ineffective Versus Effective Teacher Feedback

The important thing to remember after giving this feedback and then telling students to try again is to "close the loop" by telling your students, after their second attempt, whether they improved or not. Did they make the necessary adjustments? Are they getting there, or are they there? What should they practice, and how should they practice to get better? This second round of feedback is an essential part of the feedback loop, or complete sequential pattern (Price, 1992). In a complete rehearsal loop or sequence, the teacher sets the task for students (for example, "Play measure 6 for us"), students attempt the task (they play measure 6), and the teacher then provides *specific* feedback that enables students to understand *what to improve* ("Check your fingering for D-flat. Try it with this alternate fingering."). Research studies comparing expert and novice conductors indicate that new teachers leave out the specific feedback that completes the instructional loop and enables students to make improvements (Duke, 1999/2000; Goolsby, 1997, 1999). When you give students accurate, specific, content-related feedback and then signal them to try again to sing, play, compose, improvise ... do *not* follow their second attempt with the vague praise, "Good!" Instead, give them *more* specific feedback to keep their performance improving and increase their learning.

"Close ..."

One of the most commonly stated and *un*helpful pieces of feedback teachers say is "Close ...." The teacher asks a student a question, the student gives an inaccurate answer, the teacher does not know how to respond to the wrong answer, so the teacher says, "Close ...." Close to what? Is the answer close, or is it incorrect? If it is nearly the correct answer, tell students in what way it is close. "You told us what *crescendo* means, but the word we need to learn is *decrescendo*. How do you think putting *de* at the front of *crescendo* might change its meaning?" If the student's answer is off topic or incorrect, give specific feedback to fix it: "You guessed this word might be a dynamic marking like *crescendo*, but this word is not a dynamic; it tells us to use a bowing technique we started learning in lessons last week. Do you remember what that was?"

> **Story time:** I was observing teacher candidates teaching a lesson to third-grade students. The teacher candidates asked the class a general question (grrr), "Who can tell me an instrument that is in an orchestra?" One of the volunteer students raised his hand enthusiastically and was called on. His answer was, "Ukulele!" to which the teacher candidate said, "Close!" and moved on. Close? In what way is that close? The teacher gave the student no feedback the student could use to improve his understanding.
>
> Consider this alternative feedback: "Well, a ukulele is a stringed instrument, and the orchestra is made up of stringed instruments, so you are close.

It is possible that there is an orchestra somewhere, maybe Hawaii, that occasionally uses a ukulele, but it is not a typical orchestral instrument."

With this feedback, consider how many things you just taught the student.

First, this feedback gave an *accurate* response. Telling students that the ukulele is *not* a typical orchestral instrument, and that it is "close" to orchestra instruments because it has strings is accurate. Simply responding, "Close," suggests that the ukulele is close to a typical orchestra instrument when, in fact, it is not.

Second, this feedback was *specific*. The student would know exactly what the ukulele has to do with the orchestra: (a) that it is a string instrument, (b) that it is not typical to the orchestra, and (c) that it is associated with Hawaii.

Third, this feedback is *content-related*. The feedback is directly related to the content because it tells students what typical instruments in the orchestra are (strings), and are not (ukuleles). Because this feedback lets students know that stringed instruments are in an orchestra, it primes them to think of more specific answers to the original question.

As you can see, the feedback you give students is crucial to good teaching. Honest and specific information will help your students understand the material and feel that they are a vital part of your classroom.

CLASSROOM MANAGEMENT

One of the biggest concerns for any teacher is classroom management, which is education speech for the various techniques and processes teachers use to ensure that their classes and rehearsals run smoothly and to prevent disruptive behavior. What will you do if (when) students are off task? What should you do when a student becomes angry or aggressive? What can each teacher do to minimize off-task behavior?

The answer to most of these questions is, "It depends ...," which is not what anyone wants to hear. It does, however, depend on the needs of the particular student, the setting you are in, your strengths and weaknesses, and so on. Both experience and research (IRIS Center, 2012; Oliver, Wehby, & Reschly, 2011) indicate there are things you can do to increase your students' attention and decrease off-task behavior.

1. Set Clear and Achievable Rules and Procedures

Rules and procedures are two different things.

Rules refer to how students are to *behave*. Rules need to be

A. Limited to two to four items.

B. Clear—or written in age-appropriate language. If you teach more than one grade level, set age-appropriate rules for elementary, middle, and high school students.

C. Short—or written very briefly and clearly.

D. Written in a positive manner:

   a. Instead of "Don't talk when someone else is talking," try "Sit quietly."

   b. Instead of "Don't shout out," try "Raise your hand to speak."

E. Observable—rules need to be something the teacher can see to know whether or not they are being followed. For example, "Give 100%" is not an observable goal. "Show respect for each other" is.

F. Created with student input—at the beginning of the year, it is a very valuable use of time to have everyone give input as to the rules they think your/their class needs to have. Students are far more likely to follow rules when they have a voice in creating them.

G. Posted for everyone to see.

H. Taught, reviewed, and taught again, just like any other content.

I. Editable—if you find that a particular rule is too difficult to enforce, or you cannot model it at all times, change the rule.

You must remain consistent in making sure everyone (including you, the teacher), follows the rules, and everyone needs to know the consequences for failing to follow them. Rules should be numbered for easy reference ("Martin, you are not following rule number two."). A rule should *not* be "Show up with a pencil to class." That is a routine. Instead, rules indicate how you expect students to behave.

Routines and procedures refer to *what we are to do* when we enter or leave the classroom, how we should handle the music and/or instruments, and so on. Routines and procedures should be

A. Posted and reviewed.

B. Brief and clear.

C. A list of what everyone needs to do during transitions (entering, leaving, getting out music, putting instruments away, etc.).

D. Numbered for easy reference ("Aaron, please review procedure four—that is what you should be doing right now.").

E. Written in age-appropriate language—if you have very young students or children who do not speak English as a first language, make sure you use pictures to indicate what to do in what order.

2. Engage the Class

When students are interested and engaged in the material, they are far less likely to be off task. Choose a wide variety of music from every genre and structure lessons so that all students can succeed. Every student should be able to succeed several times in class every day. Instead of defining success by only one learning goal for each class, consider other ways you can enable students to succeed and provide specific praise to let them know they have succeeded. They may not master an entire piece of music in today's class, but they can improve in this measure, or they can get specific feedback so that they can play even one or two notes better. Lots of little successes will motivate students more effectively than one semester-long goal where success is a distant destination. Although you may have one objective for the class to learn in one period, you can engage the class in ways that give students many opportunities to succeed every day.

3. Know Yourself

Knowing what irritates you, what motivates you, what is hard for you to deal with—this knowledge gives you a greater understanding of how you will react in the classroom. Students will "push your buttons." They will notice what bothers you most, and sometimes exploit what annoys you to frustrate you and even make you angry. How you handle students' challenges to your values and patience is crucial to good teaching. You will be the only adult in the room in most cases. This means you must remain positive and professional, even in the face of stress, challenges to your authority, and immaturity. Do you have a high level of tolerance for noise? Do you notice when people are talking over someone else? I have seen many music education candidates not even notice when half of their class is talking over them while they are trying to teach. The first step toward reducing classroom noise is to pay attention to your students and notice when they talk or make noise when they should be listening. It is not good for your students to be allowed to talk when you are talking. They learn less because they are distracted, and students who are attempting to listen quietly learn less because of their peers' noise and chatter. Use class rules, procedures, and the way you structure your lessons to reduce and prevent off-task talking and noise (plucking strings, tapping, laughter, etc.),

Are you someone who gets anxious easily? Do you need to be in control to feel safe? What do you do when you feel threatened or anxious? You need to plan strategies for how to deal with these situations *before* they arise. Knowing what to expect from yourself is crucial to having a plan for your students. Where should students put their instruments when you are talking? What is one thing you will not stand for in your classroom? For example, it makes many teachers angry to see a student bullying another. As compassionate human beings, we may want to physically remove the bully or say something sarcastic or rude to the bully to put the person "in his or her place." As teachers, we have to treat the bully with respect in order to model the behavior we want to see the bully do in the future. If you think about it, it makes no sense for teachers to model bullying as a solution to bullying. However, because you may become angry and react unprofessionally, you need to find ways to deal with your own anxiety, anger, and frustrations so that you do not have to deal with them in the classroom.

4. Use Positive Classroom Management

When you phrase questions, directions, and rules in a positive manner, rather than a negative one, you focus on what your students can do—rather on what they cannot do. If I say to children, "You cannot push this button," I am focusing them on the one thing they cannot do, and often, knowing exactly what is forbidden is too enticing for immature students to resist. Instead, I could focus on the 100 other things they *can* do—read, play with a ball, do a puzzle, tell a joke, and so forth.

I often see a list of "don'ts" posted in classrooms. They are meant to be rules for the class, but, instead, they are basically a list of good ideas for students who enjoy getting off task to try. Aside from the problem of actually listing off-task behaviors, you will not be able to think of and list every single thing students must avoid doing, which becomes a nice challenge for the students: "You did not say we could not write on the walls …."

If you focus on the positive and use rules like "Respect school property," your rules will cover a wide spectrum of desired behavior without trying to make an all-inclusive list of every misbehavior students may think to do.

You should also use positive phrasing when giving directions. Instead of telling students what you do not want to see, tell them what you expect to see.

Instead of ...	Try ...
"Don't talk when I'm talking."	"Listen to others when they speak."
"I'd better not see anyone fooling around."	"I expect you to show them the same respect you show me."
"Don't chew gum."	"Leave your gum at home."
"Don't forget a pencil."	"Always bring your pencil."
"Don't play on that rest!"	"Breathe when you get to the rest."

Table 9.4: Ineffective Versus Effective Classroom Rules

In addition to making the classroom environment nicer when you focus on the positive, positive directions also state clearly what you expect. Positively stated directions are much easier than negatively stated directions for English Language Learners (ELLs) and many children with special needs to understand.

In addition, consider that what you expect from your students *must* be modeled by you. Avoid making a rule you cannot personally follow. If you cannot remember to bring all your materials to each class, do not expect your students to remember to do so. If you cannot arrive on time, do not expect them to be on time. You need to model each and every rule and expectation. Do not speak over your students if you do not want them to speak over you or anyone else. Do not make fun of or dismiss your students' music choices if you do not want them to do the same for your music. You are not only the model for their musicianship; you are also the model for their behavior. If you want them to respect you, you need to respect them. Rules must be followed by everyone in the room—that includes teachers, accompanists, students, and so on.

Persist Longer Than They Resist.

Many students who get in trouble in one class will get in trouble in all their classes. Throughout every long school day, these students hear teachers tell them what to *stop* doing. To these students, "don't" becomes background noise. Human beings tend to ignore background noise; it is just meaningless sound, like a fan or the hum of an air conditioner. Therefore, in order to have an impact on a student, use your words carefully and choose to say things that matter to *that student*. For example, you may have reason to assume that as soon as a certain student sits down, she will start to misbehave. So, as she enters the room, engage her. Tell her you like something she is wearing, or you saw her at the basketball game—whatever you need to do to start the relationship between the two of you. Frequently misbehaving students are so used to hearing negative things about themselves (even when those things are clearly a direct result of their behavior) that they are often stunned to see a teacher smile at them or to have a pleasant conversation with a teacher. You may be the only adult who gives that student a chance to say something positive.

To summarize this positive state of mind, I often say, you must "persist longer than they resist." This means you need to be positive and upbeat even when others, especially students, are disrespectful to you. You need to smile at them when they roll their eyes at you, and you need to say kind things to them when they ignore you or say unkind things to you. It might take days or weeks or even years to win over a challenging student. You never know the impact you are having on a student, negative or positive, so choose to be the guaranteed positive interaction for that child every day.

REFERENCES

Duke, R. (1999/2000). Measures of instructional effectiveness in music research. *Bulletin of the Council for Research in Music Education, 143,* 1–48. Retrieved from http://www.jstor.org/stable/40319011

Goolsby, T. W. (1997). Verbal instruction in instrumental rehearsals: A comparison of three career levels and preservice teachers. *Journal of Research in Music Education, 45,* 21–40.

Goolsby, T. W. (1999). A comparison of expert and novice music teachers' preparing identical band compositions: An operational replication. *Journal of Research in Music Education, 47,* 174–187.

The IRIS Center. (2012). *Classroom management (part 2): Developing your own comprehensive behavior management plan.* Retrieved from http://iris.peabody.vanderbilt.edu/module/beh2

Oliver, R. M., Wehby, J. H., & Reschly, D. J. (2011, June). *Teacher classroom management practices: Effects on disruptive or aggressive student behavior.* Retrieved from http://files.eric.ed.gov/fulltext/ED519160.pdf

Price, H. E. (1992). Sequential patterns of music instruction and learning to use them. *Journal of Research in Music Education, 40,* 14–29.

DISCUSSION QUESTIONS

1. Consider ways you have seen your teachers act that had a negative impact on the classroom. What could these teachers have done differently?

2. Are you the kind of student who always raises your hand and contributes to class? Do you sit back and wait to be called on? Are you assessed more or less than the other students in the class?

3. What are you most worried about when you think about classroom management and discipline? Think of strategies you can use to make sure you are treating everyone in the class with respect, even if the students do not show you respect.

4. Come up with four rules for your ideal classroom, written in a positive manner.

Image Credits

- Copyright © by Shutterstock Images LLC/all_about_people.

- Photo by Laura M. Dornberger.

- Copyright © by Shutterstock Images LLC/Pavel L. Photo and Video.

CHAPTER 10

REHEARSAL TECHNIQUES

Throughout your music educator preparation, you will learn rehearsal skills, conducting and teaching techniques, and generally how to run a classroom. When you begin leading rehearsals with students, it is likely that you will feel challenged by the common concerns discussed in this brief overview. Use these recommendations to begin building productive habits and prevent negative and ineffective habits from taking hold.

Through decades of observing student teachers and teacher candidates, I have identified several consistent problems that occur when rehearsing any ensemble. The following are the most common questions I hear from teacher candidates and my answer for each.

WHY AREN'T STUDENTS WATCHING ME?

Well ... are you giving them any *reason* to watch you? The overall goal for any conductor is to have your ensemble members watch you for cues, musicality, tempo, and so on, but without realizing it, conductors often do several things during the rehearsal that almost guarantee no one will watch them:

don't ↑ shout cues

Talking During the Rehearsal

Many new teachers shout over the ensemble to give directions in the moment. It might seem like a good idea. You assume that the ensemble members will remember what just happened, and your feedback about it, so they will

correct themselves in future rehearsals. In reality, talking over the ensemble actually creates a situation where the ensemble learns *not* to look at the conductor. Why? A new conductor gets in front of an ensemble and starts by saying, "One, two, ready, go," or by clapping, or snapping, or tapping on the stand to establish the tempo. In this case, the ensemble has no reason to watch the conductor, because they can *hear* the tempo spoken, snapped, or tapped. Why would anyone look up from their music when they can simply listen for the information while staring ahead? By making audible startup cues, the conductor unintentionally conditions the ensemble to listen instead of watch for cues. The same conditioning happens while the ensemble plays a piece of music. The conductor shouts out, "Louder, tenors!" or "You're rushing, percussion!" Once again, this audible commentary conditions the tenors and percussionists to listen, rather than watch for directions.

↳ instead cue these with hands

Eye Contact

Let's say the conductor remains silent while rehearsing the piece. Great! The conductor shows the tempo, and as soon as the piece starts, the conductor stares at the score. Once again, when players or singers watch a conductor whose head is in the score, they soon learn that there is no reason to watch. If it is appropriate for the conductor to stare at the music, why would it not be appropriate for the players to do the same thing? Look at your ensemble, and specifically at the individuals and sections that need your attention.

Know your score so well that you do not have to look down. This may be more difficult to do than you expect. Consider that the moments in any piece of music that are most complex to conduct are the moments when the music varies, for example, through *ritardandos*, *a tempi*, *fermati*, or style changes. In these moments, you can imagine that the players most need your cues; however, these will be the same moments that you will most want to consult your score! Study the score, mark important cues, and practice conducting until it is automatic. Create a score study group with friends who agree to take turns conducting scores while the others in the group sing parts and provide feedback on the clarity of the conductor's cues, styles, dynamics, and so forth.

You also need to know your score so well that you can easily identify when something is being played incorrectly. Consider your favorite song—think about it right now. If I came along and sang a note or two incorrectly, you would know right away, would you not? You know the song so well that you would immediately recognize what I did wrong. Now consider a song you have heard only once. If I sang a note or two wrong or played an incorrect rhythm in this less familiar song, you might not notice, especially if the error actually fit into the tonal center or rhythmic scheme. You need to give yourself every advantage to hear what is going on in your ensemble when you are running a rehearsal.

The other advantage to looking at your ensemble instead of the score is that you will be able to *see* errors, as well as hear them. When your eyes are on the ensemble, you are able to see the person who is not singing or playing at all, to correct students' off-task behavior, to correct playing position and embouchure, and to recognize when students are confused.

Conducting

Once you are looking at your ensemble and showing them what you want, you need to make sure your conducting is actually helpful to your ensemble. Are you in charge of the tempo, or do you follow the ensemble? Do you give a clear cue *before* they need it, or too late? Do you give cutoffs? Most new conductors I have observed do not give clear cues, and they rarely give cutoffs. The beginning of the piece needs a clear cue so that performers know exactly how to come in, and throughout the piece, including the end, performers need clear cues and cutoffs. As explained under the previous section on eye contact, if the conductor provides clear visible cues with entrances and cutoffs, the ensemble has a vested interest in watching and responding to the conducting.

What to do with that left hand? In general, unless your ensemble is so large and spread out that they cannot see your right hand, the left hand needs to do something other than mirror the right. If you keep that hand down at your side, when you lift it up, you are clearly indicating that something different is happening. The students can see this and will look up to see what is happening. Use the left hand for cues, cutoffs, phrasing, dynamics, articulation, tempo corrections, tempo changes, and so on. When you use the left hand, it should be for a reason. Give the ensemble a reason for watching you.

Mouthing the Words or Singing Along

There are several problems with mouthing words or singing along with the ensemble. First, let's look at mouthing the words when directing choirs. When you are working with young children, mouthing the words can be helpful to remind them of the lyrics. When you are working with choirs who are singing in parts, however, you need to consider that you can mouth the words for only one part. If you are mouthing the words for one part, you cannot also show the words for parts that have different rhythms. Be careful that you do not mouth words when they are not the same for everyone. If you do, you will ensure that students who sing all other parts do not watch you because you are actually showing them something that will confuse them.

Singing along with the ensemble you are conducting causes a multitude of problems for you and for your ensemble:

1. If you are singing, you cannot listen to the ensemble well because part of your listening attention is on yourself. To sing tunefully, you must listen to yourself while you sing; however, when you are conducting, you need to be diagnosing and fixing problems in the ensemble. To do that, you need to be able to hear what is happening in front of you, not your own voice. Avoid singing along so that you can hear and direct the ensemble's performance.

2. Singing along gives your students a false sense of security. There have been a number of times I have seen a group fall apart at a concert because the concert was literally the first time they had to perform without their teacher singing along! Your students need to be able to accurately assess themselves in rehearsals and to understand that they need to improve. When students rehearse without your guiding voice, they can tell that they need to improve, and they are more likely to take your feedback and apply it successfully.

3. When you are teaching full-time, you will need to use your voice quite a bit. Singing along with your ensembles hour after hour, school day after school day will damage your voice. It is just too much strain on your vocal mechanism. To maintain vocal health, you need to keep yourself hydrated and use your voice appropriately. This includes resting your voice when there is no pedagogical reason to use it.

I CANNOT GET MY STUDENTS TO STOP TALKING

The best way to stop your ensemble from talking is to give them very little opportunity to do so. Here are a few things to pay close attention to when attempting to improve your classroom management during rehearsals:

Planning

- A quick pace to the rehearsal begins with having a clear plan of what you want to accomplish and how you will accomplish it.

- Write the order of the pieces you will work on during that lesson on the board so that there is less confusion.

- Know your score and the ensemble you are rehearsing so well that you have an idea of what will go wrong and how you will fix it.

- Consider everything you and your students will need to have to make your rehearsal successful, and then make a plan for how the group will get these things. Do students need chairs set up? Who will do this? Are they allowed to talk when you are off the podium? What will you allow and require students to have at their seats during rehearsal? Will they need pencils? Can they use their phones? Must they leave phones somewhere specific?

Talking

- Speak as little as possible in your rehearsals. Surprised? Research indicates that expert conductors spend less than 55% of rehearsal time talking (Goolsby, 1997, 1999). When the amount of time that students actually make music is greater than the amount of time conductors talk, the ensemble's musical achievement is greater than it is when the majority of the rehearsal involves conductor explanations.

- When students' music-making time in rehearsal increases, their satisfaction in rehearsals increases (Napoles, 2006; see Silvey, 2014, for a review of this research). Therefore, think through the areas of your rehearsal plan that require you to

Fig. 10.1: Children learn more music by playing with brief meaningful feedback than by listening to teachers' explanations.

speak, and choose the quickest, clearest way to say what is truly necessary to enable student learning. Remember that it is more effective to *show* your students what you want them to do than it is to tell them what to do (Hewitt, 2001), so consider how you can show them as much as possible.

Feedback

- Give students specific, clear feedback quickly and get back to the music. Tell them exactly what to fix, and where to begin, then give a downbeat to make music.

- Remember to follow up on any feedback you give after the ensemble has a chance to play/sing the piece again. Did they accomplish what you wanted? Tell them. Do they still need to work on something? What? Tell them.

Involve Everyone

- Engage all sections of the group when working on something specifically with one section. If you want to work with one part of the group, what is everyone else in the room expected to do? You could have the other sections hum their own parts, listen for something specific and give feedback, or silently practice a segment they are about to play, but somehow they need to have something required of them, or they will be off task.

- Even when students in sections you are not rehearsing behave well, they learn little by sitting idly. Maximize student learning by engaging all of them in learning throughout rehearsal, *especially* when you are working with other sections. Having other parts play softly or hum their own part may also benefit the section having difficulty by enabling them to hear the context of the rest of the piece while you help them improve their parts.

Transitions

- Transitions are those times the class enters and leaves the room, gets or puts away music, changes pieces, and changes activities. These are the rehearsal moments where much off-task behavior begins. Make a plan to direct students through transitions quickly and efficiently, and keep learners engaged during transitions if possible. For example, when students walk into your room (a transition from their previous classes or socializing in the hallway), have music playing, and perhaps gesture to them to do a quick listening activity that is clearly written on the board. Put a time limit on certain transitions by counting down 5-4-3-2-1, or by playing a tune during which students get materials and get seated in their chairs before the final cadence.

- Make sure you have common class procedures posted in the room (see Chapter 9 on strategies for teaching), and refer to them often. This will make your expectations clear.

Modeling

- *Modeling* is the accepted educational term for teaching students by demonstration (Bandura, 1986). Teachers can provide models themselves or can draw students' attention to good models, such as recorded professional performances or another student's rendering of a difficult passage.

- Modeling is such a powerful teaching strategy that it teaches your students your negative and unproductive behaviors as well as your positive ones. For example, when teachers talk a lot, their students talk a lot. If you want to focus on music making instead of talking, model that.

- The fewer words you use, the more time your learners will make music, and the less time they will have to talk.

- Talk less, *do* more.

- Model the rehearsal behavior you require students to have.

I CANNOT HEAR WHAT IS WRONG OR HOW TO FIX IT

This is a common problem that worries new teachers. There is so much—music, noise, behavior, student interaction, equipment/instrument malfunctions—going on at once! It can be quite difficult to recognize exactly what went wrong and who did it, and to decide how you will fix it under the pressure of the ticking clock of limited class/rehearsal time. It may be even more difficult to think quickly of concise, effective feedback that will enable students to learn. Use these recommendations to give yourself every opportunity to hear what is happening and provide useful feedback quickly:

Prepare and Predict

- As I mentioned above, you need to make sure you know your score so well that you can hear an error, even when it is in the inner voices. This is a sure way to make error detection easier. Use your expertise to predict the errors your students might make. When you suspect something specific might go wrong, you are more likely to be able to hear that something if it actually occurs. Study your score and mark those areas you assume will be problematic for your students. Sing or play through every part so that you experience it as your students will. Perhaps the music includes tricky intervals, string crossings, or unfamiliar and complex rhythms. Maybe the notes are a bit high for the voices or instruments, or the techniques required on certain instruments will challenge the students in those sections. Your predictions will get more accurate as you gain experience.

Narrow It Down

- You may know when you hear something wrong, but you do not know where in the ensemble it happening. Choose two parts from the group to check, and cue them to sing or play. Did they make the mistake? No? Choose two different parts of the ensemble and do the procedure again. Persist!

- As previously stated, keep students learning the parts you are *not* directly rehearsing engaged in the rehearsal so that they continue learning and stay on task. Make sure that you follow up to check whatever you assigned them to do, such as humming their parts, air-playing (doing fingerings and articulations on their instruments without actually making sound), or listening for errors. Keep everyone engaged and learning!

Ask the Students

- One of your goals as a music teacher is to have students self-assess their own learning. They are the ones who are playing or singing, so ask them where the problem is. Ask them to tell you who is having a problem, and see if they can diagnose the issue.

- When you ask students to self-assess or to assess their peers' performances, make your questions specific. Asking students vague questions, such as "How did that sound?" or "How did they do?" will elicit vague responses, such as "Good ...," "We were great, but the clarinets stunk!" or, worse, responses based on individual students' popularity instead of on musical criteria. Students can assess meaningfully only when they truly understand the criteria that differentiate successful from unsuccessful performances. If they do not know what they are to judge, they will rely on the common social comparisons they make about each other daily as classmates. Andrade (2010, pp. 100–101) recommends teaching students to be self-regulated learners through the following:

  - Involving students in developing criteria for evaluating their own performances.

  - Teaching students how to use criteria to evaluate themselves and others ("You decided that posture was important for good tone. Was their posture correct? How could it have been better?").

  - Giving students appropriate feedback to their processes and products as well as their performance.

  - Guiding students in ways to use feedback and their self-assessments to improve themselves. Without this guidance, students may view assessment as the final word on their musical abilities instead of as the beginning—the information that shows them the way to improvement.

  - Providing time for students to make valid assessments and to develop knowledge and skills based on assessments. Even though they know what needs work, it may take time to improve.

  - Asking students to come up with ways they can improve in areas that assessments show to be deficient. Students often understand what they did incorrectly, but they may need your help to come up with strategies to attack the problem and make improvements.

  - Avoiding using students' self- and peer assessments to assign grades. If students sense that their honest appraisals cause negative consequences, they may feel unable to assess or mistrustful of requests that they self- or peer-assess.

- If ensemble members can articulate what they are doing incorrectly, it is likely they will be receptive to fixing the problem. If they cannot hear what is wrong, you know that you have more work to do, because your students cannot tell whether or not their performance is correct. Students' accuracy in self-evaluation tends to improve with age and experience, and students tend to evaluate their performance of melodies more accurately than their technique or articulation (Hewitt, 2001).

Proximity

- Move around the room! Walk up and down the rows of students. Get off the podium and listen as your students perform. You will hear all sorts of things you never heard from the podium. You will hear those who were not playing or singing until you neared. You will hear those who are singing or playing quietly, and you increase your chances of hearing where the errors are coming from.

- Make sure you do not move closer to students who are rehearsing as a punishment or to be intimidating. Move around the room on a regular basis, and when you do, make sure to give specific positive feedback as well as corrective feedback. If you move near students only to intimidate or criticize, your students may actually perform worse when you are near them, because they are afraid of the outcome.

- Going nearer to performing students should be an opportunity for you to give them specific feedback to either continue what they are doing, or to improve upon it.

MY ENSEMBLE KEEPS MAKING THE SAME MISTAKES OVER AND OVER AGAIN

This happens whether you are new to teaching or not, and regardless of the age of the ensemble members. The students can do it one day, and the next day they cannot do what they just fixed the previous day! Some of this vacillating is developmental, which means it is a normal part of maturing, and your students will make corrections more consistently given time to put it all together repeatedly. However, there are some things you can do to help yourself help students retain what they learn.

Feedback

- You may have noticed that this is not the first time "feedback" has appeared in this chapter. Teacher feedback is perhaps the greatest tool a teacher has for helping students learn. When you hear something that is not right, avoid saying, "Good!" and moving on. Instead, tell the students exactly what needs work, then *immediately* give them the opportunity to fix it.

Context

- So, your students can play something well when you isolate their individual parts, but as soon as you put things back into the context of the piece, they fall apart. This happens because they are not yet able to maintain their independence within the context of the piece. When students struggle because they cannot reconcile playing their rhythm against other rhythms, or singing their pitches when they hear other pitches, they need practice learning their part while hearing the other parts. Have the rest of the ensemble play their parts very quietly or hum when the students that are having difficulty are practicing, so that the struggling performers can hear a muted version of what it will sound like when they do their part in context. Once the struggling group succeeds with the other parts at muted volume, repeat the process with the other parts, increasing their volume one level. Continue until all parts are balanced and dynamically appropriate.

- Avoid becoming alarmed or angry with students when their performance causes you to repeat feedback and rehearsal techniques that were worked on in a previous successful lesson. Music making requires coordination of complex thought, concentration, memory, and motor skills, and growing students' minds and bodies change rapidly. Retention of new learning requires practice and motivation. Persist more than they resist!

Authentic Assessment

- Here is a mistake many conductors make: You sing or play along with a group to help them learn a piece, and they get it right! Great! However, the next time you rehearse with them, they can no longer do what they did correctly before. What happened? Actually, the group was never able to perform the music correctly on their own, but you thought they could because your assessment (your decision as to whether or not they understood the content) was inauthentic. You assessed the group's performance when you sang or played along with them, not when they performed on their own. To authentically assess the group's ability to perform alone, you needed to hear them perform *without* your singing or playing.

- When you listen to your students to assess their understanding, be sure that you are listening authentically—that you are listening for the exact performance skills, student answers, signs of understanding—in the exact conditions (for example, unaccompanied, alone or within an ensemble, giving written answers or verbal answers) that you intend to assess.

Practice

- Maybe your students really did understand the content the last time they played/sang it for you. Maybe you thoughtfully avoided singing or playing along with them, and maybe you *did* give specific feedback in context, but your ensemble members still cannot do it the next time you see them. Then the next question to ask yourself is how much time did you spend in your rehearsals teaching students how to practice? You may spend some time teaching practice strategies in group lessons, but how much rehearsal time do you spend on it? What strategies do you give them for taking home the music after rehearsal and practicing it to ensure that they can play it correctly the next time? "Practice that part!" is not a useful direction because it is too vague. When students take music home and do not know how to practice efficiently or correctly, they will either practice the music the way they first did it (incorrectly), or they will practice only the parts they can already play correctly (McPherson & Renwick, 2001; Renwick & McPherson, 2002). Consider how many times you, as a musician, sit down to practice your primary instrument, or perhaps a secondary instrument like piano, and find yourself playing the parts you can do well instead of working on the parts you cannot play. That's because people do not like making music that sounds bad. Considering that you are an educated musician, and you do this, imagine how prevalent it is for children to practice only what sounds good. Take the time to give students specific, targeted strategies to practice what they need to improve. Tell them to enjoy playing music they already know at the end of their sessions as a reward for making progress on the parts they find difficult.

If you begin rehearsing with these strategies in mind, you will improve your chances of having an effective rehearsal. The good news is that children are predictable. We know the kinds of mistakes they will make and the areas of rehearsal that are likely to be problems for them before we enter the rehearsal room. Planning for the mistakes students are likely to make and making improvements to your personal approaches to teaching will go a long way toward creating the kind of atmosphere in which all children can be successful and grow as musicians.

REFERENCES

Andrade, H. L. (2010). Students as the definitive source of formative assessment: Academic self-assessment and the self-regulation of learning. In H. L. Andrade & G J. Cizek (Eds.), *Handbook of formative assessment* (pp. 91, 94, 100–101). New York, NY: Routledge.

Bandura, A. (1986). *Social foundations of thought and action: A social cognitive theory*. Englewood Cliffs, NJ: Prentice Hall.

Goolsby, T. W. (1997). Verbal instruction in instrumental rehearsals: A comparison of three career levels and preservice teachers. *Journal of Research in Music Education, 45,* 21–40.

Goolsby, T. W. (1999). A comparison of expert and novice music teachers' preparing identical band compositions: An operational replication. *Journal of Research in Music Education, 47,* 174–187.

Hewitt, M. P. (2001). The effects of modeling, self-evaluation, and self-listening on junior high instrumentalist's music performance and practice attitude. *Journal of Research in Music Education, 49*(4), 307–322.

McPherson, G. E., & Renwick, J. M. (2001). A longitudinal study of self-regulation in children's musical practice. *Music Education Research, 3*(2), 169–186.

Napoles, J. (2006). The effect of duration of teacher talk on the attitude, attentiveness, and performance achievement of high school choral students. *Research Perspectives in Music Education, 11*, 22–29.

Renwick, J. M., & McPherson, G. E. (2002). Interest and choice: Student-selected repertoire and its effect on practicing behavior. *British Journal of Music Education, 19*(2), 173–188.

Silvey, B. A. (2014). Strategies for improving rehearsal technique: Using research findings to promote better rehearsals. *UPDATE: Applications of Research in Music Education, 32*(2), 11–17. doi: 10.1177/8755123313502348

RECOMMENDED READING

Ali, S. (2010). Understanding our students' self-regulation during practice: Verbal protocol as a tool. *Journal of Singing, 66*(5), 529–536.

Miksza, P. (2011). A review of research on practicing: Summary and synthesis of the extant research with implications for a new theoretical orientation. *Bulletin of the Council for Research in Music Education, 190*, 51–92.

DISCUSSION QUESTIONS

1. Think of a conductor with whom you have worked. What specific techniques did that conductor use to run a rehearsal that worked well?

2. Have you been in a rehearsal where you were bored or where you felt your time was wasted? What can you do to avoid putting your students in a similar situation?

3. What have you wished your conductors would have done or refrained from doing during rehearsals to help you and your peers?

Image Credits

- Copyright © 2016 by Thomas Dornberger. Reprinted with permission.

- Copyright © by Shutterstock Images LLC/TZIDO SUN.

- Fig. 10.1: Copyright © by Depositphotos/photographee.eu.

- Copyright © 2013 by Shutterstock Images LLC/cemT.

CHAPTER 11

MAKING OBSERVATIONS MEANINGFUL

Throughout your music educator preparation, you will observe many music teachers working with children. Many times the teachers you observe will give you the opportunity to teach and rehearse a little, but you can gain a wealth of knowledge from observing them working. Watching and listening to teachers can teach you a great deal if you know what to notice.

Schools must maintain the safety of the children and staff members in the building; therefore, you must contact school officials to arrange permission to visit classes when children are present. You must get permission to visit from school officials even if you know the school's music teachers, you attended the school yourself, or your brothers, sisters, or other relatives attend classes there. Expect to be required to provide school office staff with official forms from your university or college indicating that you are in an educator preparation program that requires you to complete observations. Expect to present photo identification of yourself when you arrive at the school each day you observe, and to sign yourself in and out in the school's office. Some school districts require additional measures, such as brief interviews with administrators, recommendations from your university's music education program head, or that your fingerprints be on file in the state's system (fingerprinting is a standard requirement for teacher certification in many states).

When you receive permission to visit, be sure to ask where you are allowed to park your vehicle or which public transportation routes will get you to the school site. Find out the exact hours of the school day, and ask whether or not there are any special events during your observations, such as school concerts, assemblies, or field trips that will affect the children's attendance in music classes or the music teacher's schedule during your visit.

When you observe school music programs, arrive at the school building at least 30 minutes before the time of the first class you are scheduled to observe to allow yourself time to sign in on a busy morning in the school office. Expect to be required to wear a visible visitor's badge. Put it on and comply with all school policies throughout your visit. You should arrive dressed as a *teacher*, not as a student. Consider that you may need to move around on the floor with young children if you observe general music classes, and that you may need to lean over in front of adolescents to reposition cellists' bows or demonstrate abdominal breathing to high school choir members, all while looking professional. If your age is within 10 years of the age of the high school students you may observe, it is especially important that you avoid looking like the students. You must own your new role as a teacher and set aside your past role as a high school student. As a future educator and authorized observer in the school, you are, during your visit, part of the team entrusted with the safety of every student you meet during your observations. Students' safety includes safety from any sexual conduct, interest, or action from you or any other adults. Students may feel that you are approachable in ways that a peer is approachable. You are *not*, and the law is clear concerning your responsibilities as an adult teacher-in-training school visitor. Dress, act, and conduct yourself professionally at all times.

WHAT TO OBSERVE WHEN YOU ARE OBSERVING

The paperwork is signed, your schedule is set, your professional attire and transportation plans are ready, you have a notebook and pens ready for note taking, and the day to begin your observation finally arrives. What should you notice to learn the most from this opportunity?

CLASSROOM ARRANGEMENT

Much of the time, there is little teachers can do to improve the physical constraints of their classrooms (if they even *have* a dedicated music classroom or rehearsal space). They are assigned a room, and they need to work with it the best they can. As a new person to the room, you may be able to think of some ways in which the setup could be improved. Make a note of anything in the room that you would like to have when you get a music room of your own, and consider the following:

- Does the teacher have a dedicated music room, or does the music class meet in a common space (cafeteria, auditorium, hallway)?

- Is there room for students to move around?

- How is the room organized?

- Is there a good flow to the room's setup, so that students can get in, get music and instruments, and be seated without crossing each other's paths repeatedly?

- Could you envision the room working better if it were set up differently? Sketch your preferred setup ideas in your notes.

- What equipment and/or technology does the teacher have in the room that helps him or her teach?

- Is there any equipment the teacher does not have that you would want in your classroom?

ORGANIZATION

The way teachers organize their classes makes a big difference in how lessons or classes go. When the students enter the class, they should know where to go, what to do, and what is expected of them.

- Is there music playing as the students enter? If so, what do you notice about the music? Tempo? Relation to the lesson? Instructions?

- In what ways does the teacher run the actual class? How does the teacher get students to move from activity to activity, to get music or instruments, or to get into groups?

- What procedures do the students follow as they enter and leave the room?

- Are procedures posted in the room? What are they?

- How do the students take out their instruments or pick up their music folders?

- Is there a specific routine to begin and/or end the class? If so, is there a different routine for different age students or for different ensembles and lessons?

- Does the classroom organization plan work well, or can you think of changes that would make it run more smoothly?

CLASSROOM MANAGEMENT

You should be able to quickly tell how effective the teacher's class management is. The way teachers react to all students and the way the students respond to teachers, to each other, and to you are all indicators that they are used to clear communication and expectations (or not).

- Are there rules posted? What are they?

- Are the rules actually rules for how students are to behave, or are they procedures for what students are to do?

- Are the rules written in a positive or negative manner?

- Does the teacher ever refer to the posted rules when there is an issue with students' behavior or cooperation?

- Does the teacher call out students for doing something wrong, or does the teacher focus on redirecting off-task students and praising on-task students?

- Does the teacher yell at the class?

- Does the teacher threaten the class with punishment or lower grades?

- Does the teacher use extrinsic motivators like rewards (stickers, prizes, etc.)?

- Does the teacher seem to expect students to behave, or does it seem like the teacher expects the students to misbehave?

- Does the teacher smile, motivate, compliment, and seem to generally enjoy teaching?

FEEDBACK

What kind of feedback does the teacher provide to students throughout the lesson? Teacher feedback should be specific, helpful, and honest.

- Is there a phrase that the teacher repeats often, such as "good," "good job," or "not quite"?

- How long does it take the teacher to give feedback? Truly! Count seconds in your mind as you listen. Does feedback take 10 seconds, 15 seconds, a minute? Does the duration of the teacher's feedback vary with students' age or grade?

- Does the teacher give the students an opportunity to implement the feedback and try again?

- When the teacher gives feedback, does she or he provide enough information for the students to know what they did wrong and how to fix it?

- Does the feedback provided address only behavioral issues, or does it also address musical issues?

- Does the teacher provide the students with opportunities to supply their own feedback for either their own work or others' work?

REHEARSAL TECHNIQUES

When you watch a teacher run a rehearsal, there are many things to listen and notice. You will also learn a lot from watching your college conductors, but you have to keep in mind that those conductors are working with college musicians, and therefore not all their techniques will be applicable to children. When you watch a teacher rehearsing children in an ensemble, try to predict what the conductor will say when they stop the ensemble, and see if you can come up with a way to fix the problem before the teacher says it.

- How long does the ensemble play before being stopped? Seconds? Minutes? Longer?

- How long does the teacher talk in the intervals when the ensemble is stopped before having the students play again?

- How many times does the teacher work with children during rehearsal on how to sing or how to play the instruments?

- What kind of feedback does the teacher give the students?

- Does the teacher reprimand students who are not playing well or reprimand an entire section?

- Does the teacher give the students an opportunity to give feedback on what they hear?

- Does the teacher provide the students with the opportunity to fix their own mistakes? How can you tell whether this occurs? Does the teacher actually remind or ask students to self-correct, or do students seem to self-correct automatically during repeated playing? Do you notice students repeating errors without correction? What kinds of errors do you hear them make?

- Does the teacher offer students opportunities to choose the music they play?

PACING

If the lesson's or rehearsal's pacing is too slow, students become bored, and there is a lot of down time, which may cause some students to misbehave or stray from on-task learning. If the lesson's or rehearsal's pacing is too quick, students become lost and frustrated, which also can cause students to misbehave. When teachers' pacing is quick and the difficulty of the tasks and activities is appropriate for the class or group, the students have little opportunity to get off task, and there is a positive energy and a sense of accomplishment for everyone in the room.

- Who seems busier, the teacher or the students?

- Does the teacher talk a lot, or are students actively participating throughout the class or rehearsal?

- Does the teacher seem to know what is coming next, or does the teacher take time to find materials or consult the lesson plan?

- Does the teacher seem to motivate the students to keep working, or do the students seem to be setting the pace?

- Does the teacher provide the students with specific directions that help with pacing, such as, "Come up to the front of the room quickly and quietly"?

PHILOSOPHY

You can tell a lot about a teacher's philosophy by looking for all of the above information. Pay closer attention to what you see teachers do than to what they say they believe.

- What does the teacher believe about children based on what you have observed? For example, does the teacher seem to believe that *all* students can be musicians?

- Which does the teacher seem to value more: students' experiences making music, or the perfection of the music being performed?

- Does the teacher think children are capable of a lot, or generally incapable? (Teachers who always do things for their students, assume that students will misbehave, or expect very little from the students show, by their actions, that they believe children to be incapable.)

- What kind of music does the teacher select for general music and ensembles? Based on the music selections, does this teacher believe that all music is valuable to teach, or only certain kinds of music?

- Do students have leadership roles in the music program? Do they get a voice in what kind of music they perform? Do they have responsibilities within the music program?

- What does the music room look like? Are there motivational posters? Colorful signs? Decorations?

METHODS

- Do you recognize any music teaching methods that are being used (e.g., Orff, Kodaly, Music Learning Theory)?

- What counting system does the teacher use with the students?

- Do the students use solfège? Hand signs? If yes, is C always "Do" (fixed Do), or does "Do" change to the home tone of any key (moveable Do)?

- Do the students sing or play instruments in modes other than major? If they use solfège, do they use La-based minor or Do-based minor?

STUDENTS WITH SPECIAL NEEDS

Hammel and Hourigan (2011) recommend completing systematic observations of music classes that include students with special needs. They recommend focusing your observations on each of five disability categories: cognitive, communication, behavioral and emotional, physical, and sensory (pp. 13–20).

- Does the teacher present information in different modes (visual, aural, kinesthetic) to teach students with different sensitivities?

- Does the teacher accept different assessments from different students (written from one, verbal from another)?

- What behavioral strategies does the teacher use? Are there any noticeable triggers related to negative or positive student behaviors?

- What communication strategies does the teacher use to accommodate learners (simplified language, songs, pictures, gestures)?

- Are there English langauge learners in the class? What strategies does the teacher use to help these learners understand (labels in child's first language, visual aids, study aids)?

REFERENCE

Hammel, A., & Hourigan, R. (2011). *Teaching music to students with special needs: A label-free approach.* New York, NY: Oxford University Press.

Image Credit

- Photo by Laura M. Dornberger.

CHAPTER 12

INTERVIEWING TECHNIQUES

So, you are now the most informed, well-rounded, motivated, and educated teacher ever! Now you are ready to get a job. ... The good news is that practicing and understanding how to interview for jobs will help improve your skills and make getting a job easier. I have done many workshops and training events on interviewing skills, and I have interviewed literally hundreds of candidates, which makes me uniquely qualified to offer advice to you on this topic. There are certain things you *never* say in an interview and other things you want to make sure to include, so that when the door closes, and you leave the interview behind, the interview panel talks about how impressed they were with you and how much they want to hire you!

THE PROBLEM

The biggest problem you face as you enter any interview is that you don't have much teaching experience yet. Understanding this problem can be the key to getting a job. The good news is that your competition will be mostly other inexperienced teacher candidates, and you are cheap labor right out of college. Interviewers will assume that you will take feedback well because you have just been a student, and that you will understand the latest trends in education, and that you will be eager to become an integral part of their school community. Also, they *know* that you have no experience based on your résumé, so if they have asked you for an interview, clearly your lack of experience isn't that big of a deal to them.

Why is lack of experience a problem, then? To most experienced, older professionals, inexperience equals immaturity, and no one wants to work with immature teachers. To overcome this problem, you need to make sure that you are the most professional and mature candidate they see all day. Some things to think about:

- Be early: Be in the building 15 minutes early for your interview. Be far earlier to the parking lot so that you can stop sweating, blow your nose, breathe, and so on.

- Dress professionally: Wear conservative, professional attire. Iron your clothes, and tuck in your shirt; men should wear a tie and a jacket. Do not wear perfume or cologne—it can be overwhelming in a small space.

- Make sure you have a professional e-mail address, instead of one that makes you appear immature or amateur.

- Leave your phone off or in the car.

- Make sure all social media sites of yours are something you would not be embarrassed to show potential employers.

- Your hair should, of course, be well groomed and clean, and it also should be out of your face.

- Jewelry should not be so much as to make excessive noise when you move or distracting to yourself. (If you fidget with your rings, do not wear rings.)

- Take social cues from the interviewers. If they do not extend a hand to you, do not extend one to them. Often in school situations, the interview panel will skip hand shaking so that they don't spread germs.

- Sit still. Sit up in the chair, remain still, and look at all your interviewers in the eyes. Good eye contact can really set you apart from the rest of the field, and it also makes you seem more confident. Look at *everyone* on the panel, not just the person who asked the question. Remember, the interview panel is going to assume (rightly or wrongly) that however you answer these questions is how you will behave when you are the teacher. Will you look at only the student who asked you the question, or will you address the entire class in a way that includes everyone?

- Know your audience: Pay attention to titles, more than names, when the members of the panel introduce themselves. A parent, English teacher, principal, assistant principal, and music teacher are each going to want to hear different things from you. Knowing who is in the room can be an advantage when you answer questions about discipline, motivation, creativity, cross-curricular ideas, and so forth. You can focus your answers more toward the individuals in the room who you know care most about those issues.

Fig. 12.1: Sit still. Sit up in the chair and make eye contact. Dress professionally and modestly.

- Research the school and community. There is no excuse not to know quite a bit about the community and school district in which you are interviewing. Look up the size of the school and the number of students and teachers. Look at the school website for pictures of the facilities, a list of ensembles, school-wide initiatives the staff may be involved with—things you can bring up in an interview that show that you are interested and enthusiastic about this job. Your research can enable you to ask pertinent questions: "I see you have a jazz band—does that meet at the same time as band/chorus, or are students able to be in both groups?"

KNOW YOURSELF

This and all other steps really stem from the first one—the problem of having little teaching experience. Remember that in order to battle that problem, you need to show your maturity, and mature professional teachers understand their strengths and weaknesses. You need to think this through before any interview. I tell my workshop attendees/students that every question in an interview can be separated into one of three categories:

1. What are you like as a person?
    Will you fit in with the rest of the faculty? Do you seem like someone with whom the rest of us would like to spend the next 30 years? In other words ... do we like you?

2. What are you like as a teacher?
    Are you a good teacher? Can you take a large amount of information and break it down to understandable parts? Will you be a good colleague who can manage a classroom without sending your students to the principal's office? Are you motivating and engaging?

3. What are your skills as a musician?
    Are you a talented musician who will serve as an excellent musical role model for our students? Are you able to teach and play a wide variety of styles and instruments? What kind of music will you be teaching our students?

If you break down any question you will be asked in an interview, it will fall into one of those three categories: person, teacher, and musician. To prepare for an interview, then, you need to ask yourself questions in each of these categories so that you have an idea of the kind of music teacher you are turning out to be. Having thought through these questions, you will be far more likely to be successful at interviewing (see the worksheet at the end of this chapter).

Tell Us About Yourself ...

The first question is always something similar to *"Tell us about yourself."* This is the same question as "Who are you?" "Why are you the right fit for this job?" and other open-ended questions about yourself. These questions are good ways to begin an interview, because your answer shows the panel of interviewers a lot about who you are right from the start. Remember that your interviewers will interpret everything they see and hear you say in an interview through the lens of a teacher. It is no coincidence that this first question is open-ended. They are asking you to break down a large amount of information (your entire life), and put it into a comprehensive explanation in which you *teach* them about you. Of course, this is exactly what you will be doing when you are teaching music—you will take the vast amount of information from an enormous subject (music), and create lessons. What you choose to say and what you choose *not* to say will tell the interviewers quite a bit about your teaching style. If you ramble on for ten minutes about every detail you can think of, they will assume that is how you will teach. On the other end of the spectrum, if all you say is what your name is and where you went to school (which they can read on your résumé), they can only conclude that this is how you will teach your students—tersely, with no explanations or expansions to make the content interesting.

The best way to answer this first open-ended question is to say something unique about yourself and then explain how what you said about yourself makes you a better candidate *for that specific job* than anyone else. For example, if you tell the interview panel that you like to knit, it does not tell them much. If, however, you tell the panel that you love to knit, so if given the opportunity, you would love to start a knitting club for faculty, or teach students and faculty after school, or even incorporate that hobby into

Fig. 12.2: Hello! Tell us about yourself.

fundraising for the music department, you connect your interests to their school so that the panel can get excited about how thoughtful and involved you will be as a teacher in their district. Just talking about yourself is not the strongest answer. Instead, do your best to connect the information to your audience (what can you do for *them*?).

I once asked a candidate if her piano skills were strong enough to help accompany the chorus. Her answer was "No." That was the entire answer. Although it is crucial to be honest and to make sure the interviewers know that piano is not your strength if indeed it is not, this particular individual's negative piano answer was the sole reason she did not get the job. Why? How would you answer this question?

The best way to answer a question about a qualification that is a weakness is to be honest about your skills and then follow up with other ways you could fulfill the school's needs. In the case of piano skills, your answer could explain other ways you could assist the chorus. For example, "My piano skills would not be strong enough to accompany the choir, but my main instrument is French horn, and I would be happy to write a part and play with the choir on the French horn," or "I also play several other instruments. I would love to have some of my band students work on accompaniment parts—composing and performing them with the choir. If all else fails, I would be more than happy to help with crowd control at choir functions, lining them up, handing out materials, etc." This answer gives the interview panel so many other ideas. They may start thinking how creative, thoughtful, and talented you are, rather than wishing you played piano better. They can *see* you in this position already, and they can tell that you see yourself there, too. This answer also demonstrates your ability to work with other people, to find creative solutions to problems, to be a team player, and that you understand the many different needs of a music program. You also would have just demonstrated that you understand how important it is for your band students to compose and to collaborate—very important skills for musicians!

STRENGTHS AND WEAKNESSES

A common question you may get is *"What is your greatest strength and biggest weakness?"* A little trick I teach my students is to reverse this. Start with your weakness. Make sure it is an actual weakness (do not say, "I just care too much about my students," because the entire panel will roll their eyes), and then explain how you are addressing it. Perhaps your biggest weakness is your lack of piano skills. Make sure you then say how you are getting better (you are taking lessons, working on it, have someone who will play at concerts for you, etc.). After you talk about your *one* weakness (they asked for only one of each, so give them only one of each), finish strongly with your greatest strength. It leaves your interviewers on a positive note, and very savvy interview panels will be impressed that you thought to end on your strength in a stressful situation like an interview.

It is acceptable to pause briefly before you answer any interview question, but it is not effective to say, "Uh ...," "Um ...," or "Hmm ... ." These stumbling, pausing sounds make you seem very unsure, and although you may be very unsure, you do not want the panel to know that. Common things candidates do to stall are to compliment the interviewer on the question, repeat the question, say, "I have never thought of that before," or insert the above "umm" placeholders. Instead, pause briefly, look at the interviewers, and answer confidently. Again, whether it is fair or not, the evidence the panel members have to decide what kind of a teacher you will be is based on how you answer these questions. Teachers answer a lot of questions, so you need to demonstrate how well you can do that.

It is far easier to get a job when you have never had one than it is to get a job when you have been let go or fired from one. Make good choices from the beginning. Is the position for which you are applying a good fit for your skill set and personality? You might not know going in to the interview if the position is a good fit, but you might have some idea based on your knowledge of the school district and the job description. If you can see from the job description that strong piano skills are needed and you do not have strong piano skills, do not apply for the job. I have seen many situations where a candidate lied about his or her abilities, only to get into the job and fail in it. That failure is bad for you and your résumé, it is bad for the school, and it is bad for the children. If the school needs someone with skills you do not have, they would not be happy with you, and you would not be happy with them. Always be honest about your skill level.

QUESTIONS FOR THEM

Often at the end of an interview, the panel will ask you if you have any questions for them. This may be your only opportunity to ask them anything. First, let me tell you what *not* to ask them. Do not ask them about money. Schools do not operate like businesses. You are not going to be able to negotiate a salary, so it does not matter much anyway. If you are hired, you will be entering the school's payroll scale on a "step" that has already been negotiated in the district based on your education and experience. This is something to talk about in your very final interview, most likely with the superintendent or principal alone. The salary question also makes you seem as though money is the only thing on your mind. Instead, ask the panel questions that once again show them that you are interested in their district. You can pose questions such as these:

- What opportunities are there for a new teacher to become involved in the school community?

- Is there a mentoring program for new teachers?

- What is the district's policy on mainstreaming and inclusion?

- Do teachers participate in curriculum review and change?

ILLEGAL QUESTIONS

No employer can legally ask you questions regarding your race, gender, sexual preference, religion, marital status, age, physical and/or mental disabilities, ethnic background, or country of origin. However, this does not mean that it does not happen. The interviewers may ask illegal questions, especially during transition times when you are all sitting waiting for someone to arrive. I have seen several instances where someone on the panel says something like "Wow—it's Ash Wednesday ... Are you Catholic?" or "Do you have a husband?" trying to make small talk. These are illegal questions. You have three options if you are asked an illegal question:

1. Answer the question. It is not illegal for you to answer the question. If you do not mind, and if you think it was an honest mistake, you could choose to answer it.

2. Refuse to answer the question. Say something like "I am sorry; that is not a legal question, and I do not feel comfortable answering it." You may also want to report the incident to the state's education department. If the very first time you are interacting with this school district, they ask you something illegal, it may not be the best place to work anyway.

3. Address the information behind the question. If someone asks you, "Do you plan to settle down and have children?" it is an illegal question. If you wanted to address the concern behind that question, you may choose to answer it like this: "I understand your concern, and I want to assure you that if I get this job, I will remain here, making this school and community my top priorities." I did not answer the illegal question, but I did address the underlying concern, which is to ask whether I am going to stick around for the long term, or if I will be looking to move on or quit. Again, you may later decide you don't want to work for a district that asked you an illegal interview question, but if you feel it was an honest mistake, and everything else went well, this response is an option to take without actually answering the offending question.

FREQUENTLY ASKED QUESTIONS

Here are the most popular questions I am asked when I do workshops on interviewing:

If I Am Late for the Interview, Should I Even Bother Showing Up?

Short answer: Yes.

Longer answer: Because you are late, you probably will not get the job. How you handle it, however, could harm your chances of getting a job at a neighboring district. Make sure you call as soon as you know you will be late and tell them when you think you will arrive. It is possible they will tell you not to bother, but in most cases, if you are only going to be a few minutes late, they will still allow you to interview. When you arrive, be apologetic and let them know that you realize what a big deal it is to be late to an interview. It's important for them to know that you do not think this is acceptable behavior. Everyone else was on time or early for their interview and you were not—it does not look good for this job, but you did what you could, and at least you showed them your character. Send a note after the interview, once again apologizing and thanking them for allowing you to interview. When another job becomes available in that district or another, at least you will be considered, because you handled your mistake as well as you could.

I Have a Tattoo/Nose Ring/Lip Ring—Should I Take It Out or Cover It Up?

Short answer: There is no short answer.

Longer answer: If you are going to wear that nose ring every day, and it is part of who you are, wear it to the interview. If they do not hire you because of it, you would not have been happy working there anyway. If, however, it does not really matter to you to wear the ring daily, I recommend taking it out for the interview. If you do get the job, you can always ask a mentor if it would be alright to wear it or not. The same thing applies to covering a tattoo or not. You want there to be a good match between you and the district. Be honest. Although you need to present your best self, you still need to be *yourself*.

I Am Sure I Will Only Be in This Job for a Year or Two. When They Ask Me Where I See Myself in 5 or 10 Years, Should I Lie and Say I Want to Be Still Teaching at This District, or Should I Be Honest?

Short answer: Do not lie.

Longer answer: Honestly, you have no idea where you will be in 5 or 10 years. You do not know that you will work for a couple of years and then go to graduate school full-time. It may be your plan, but there is no guarantee. It is hard to walk away from a full-time job with good pay and benefits once you have it. You might as well be generally honest and tell them that you see yourself happy and teaching in a district where you can make a difference.

Should I Mention Organizations of Which I Am a Part That Will Indicate My Religion, Politics, or Sexual Identity?

Short answer: It depends ...

Longer answer: First, ask yourself why you are thinking of mentioning it. Are you simply listing your interests? Then you really do not have a great reason to mention it. Do you hold a position of leadership within the organization? Did you achieve something through that organization? If so, perhaps you do want to mention it as an example of your breadth of experiences and the quality of your work. Consider this, though—when you talk about religion and politics, you immediately alienate roughly 50% of your audience. The panel cannot legally ask you about any of the above, so when you offer this information, there should be a good reason. Again, if you say something that shows your political leanings, and that information makes them not hire you, you would not have been happy in the position or in that district.

What Should I Bring With Me to the Interview?

Short answer: Whatever the district asks you to bring.

Longer answer: Normally you would ask what they want you to bring when you make plans to come in for the interview. If they are not specific and you just want to be sure, bring some more copies of your résumé, any video you have of your teaching or conducting, and any portfolio you have of your work. This way, if they ask, you have it, and if they do not ask, you were well prepared.

I Happen to Know Someone in the District. Should I Drop That Name in the Interview?

Short answer: No.

Longer answer: *No.* I have never experienced an interview panel that is impressed with name-dropping. It does not make a good impression. If someone has put in a good word for you, great—let that person do it, but stick to showing the interviewers who you are and how you teach, not who you know.

Do Women Need to Wear a Skirt or Dress, and Do Men Need to Wear a Jacket and Tie?

Short answer: No and yes.

Longer answer: Women do not have to wear a skirt or a dress. As long as you are dressed very professionally, pants or a pantsuit are absolutely fine. In fact, pants are preferred if you would otherwise wear a skirt and then fidget with it during the interview. As for men, yes, they should wear a jacket and a tie. I have found that men can also wear fun musical ties, as long as they are still professional.

Is There Such a Thing as Too Much Jewelry?

Short answer: Yes.

Longer answer: Remember that the interview panel is trying to determine what kind of a teacher you will be based on what they see during your interview. When you wear, for example, a large number of bracelets that make quite a bit of noise when you move, the interview panel is left with the impression that you do not understand how that could be very distracting for children, especially children with special needs. If it would be distracting for those who are listening to you and watching you, leave it at home.

Does It Matter How I Wear My Hair?

Short answer: Yes.

Longer answer: Although it does not matter to the interview panel if you wear your hair down or up, it does matter if your hair is in your eyes or if you play with your hair or have to move it when you talk. Your hair should not be a distraction. The panel should be able to see your full face, and you need to look confident and mature, which you won't if you are playing with your hair.

Can I Wear My Favorite Perfume/Cologne?

Short answer: No.

Longer answer: Do not do it. Refrain from wearing any scents. Once again, the interview panel is looking to see what kind of a teacher and colleague you will be. When you are working with a group of people in a small, confined space, you need to consider that scents can negatively impact other people. Many people are allergic or sensitive to scents. Show them that you are considerate of a wide range of people by avoiding scents until you get to know district policies and your individual students and colleagues.

My Biggest Awards Accomplishments Occurred When I Was in High School. Should I Mention Those?

Short answer: No, unless you really have to.

Longer answer: Remember that the main weakness new teachers have is that they lack experience and they are young. You want to do everything you can to show how mature you are. When you talk a lot about your high school accomplishments, it serves as a strong reminder of how young you are and how recently it was that you were in high school. In most cases, an award in high school would be for performing, not teaching, so it is not as relevant to the job as you may think it is. If, however, you traveled extensively with an honor band or chorus, or went on a mission trip to another country, these experiences show you are probably more mature than most other candidates of the same age. Mention them, but phrase it that "four years ago" you did this, rather than "in high school."

Should I Send a Thank-You Letter After My Interview?

Short answer: Yes.

Longer answer: Pay attention to the main way the district communicated to you. Was it mainly or entirely through e-mail? If so, an e-mail of thanks is sufficient. If they always communicated through the phone or by mail, you will want to write a thank-you note and mail it to them. Be specific with your thank-you note. Thank the interviewers for their time and attention and try to remind them who you are. Mention something that was specific to your interview, follow up with any information they requested, and so on. Give them the clear impression that you are a great teacher who is specific with feedback.

QUESTIONS TO PREPARE

Answer these questions before attempting to interview. If you have a good idea of how you will answer these questions, you will be more confident and able to ace any interview.

Who am I as a person?

Why do I want to this *particular* job?

How would I describe myself in one word?

What is my greatest strength? Greatest weakness? How do I work on that weakness?

What is unique about me?

What is one thing I want the interview panel to know about me?

Is there a struggle that I have overcome that I am willing to discuss with the panel?

How do I resolve conflicts with others? Do I have an example of a conflict I was able to resolve?

What can I contribute to this *particular* district and community?

How do I want my students, colleagues, and principal to describe me?

What goals do I have for a music program?

What/who is my favorite food/book/movie/TV show/pop musician/composer?

Who am I as a teacher?

What do I like about teaching?

What do I like about children?

What is my philosophy of music education?

What is my greatest strength as a teacher?

What do I struggle with when planning, teaching, and/or assessing?

What grade level do I see myself teaching? Why? What grade level do I least enjoy teaching? Why?

How do I describe my teaching style?

How do I check for understanding during a lesson—individually and class-wide?

How do I describe my classroom management? How do I motivate and maintain class interest and discipline?

How do I accommodate the needs of diverse learners?

Who am I as a musician?

Which secondary instruments do I know well, and which less well? How will I meet my students' needs?

How do I describe my piano skills? How will I meet this need in teaching and/or concerts?

What type of music do I think should be included in my classroom?

How do I determine what good music is?

How do I determine whether a concert is a success?

What do I see as my primary job as music teacher? Is it to teach music reading? Inspire? Provide experiences?

What materials would I need to be successful in this job?

What is the current musical climate in the district? (Make sure you look this up ahead of time.)

How do I describe my singing skills? My sight-reading skills? What if I have to sing a song?

Do I have a video or recording of me performing and/or teaching? (Choose the clip wisely.) What does this clip highlight about me as a teacher, conductor, and/or musician?

Image Credits

- Fig. 12.1: Copyright © by Shutterstock Images LLC/OPOLJA.

- Fig. 12.2: Copyright © by Shutterstock Images LLC/StockLite.

- Copyright © 2016 by Thomas Dornberger. Reprinted with permission.

ABOUT THE AUTHORS

Laura M. Dornberger

Laura M. Dornberger serves on the music education faculty at the State University of New York at Fredonia. Her teaching credits include student teaching supervision as well as graduate and undergraduate courses in elementary general music methods, child development, philosophy of music education, assessment, and *Music, Play, & Self*, a Liberal Arts course. Before coming to Fredonia, Laura Dornberger taught PK-12th grade general/vocal music, directed children's choirs, performed professionally as a soprano, and taught private voice and piano lessons for ten years. She contributed as a panelist to numerous teacher hiring committees where she gained insights on interviewing from administrators' perspectives. She led workshops on the use of music for learner engagement and support for teachers in Cork, Ireland. She serves as a scorer for the New York State Teacher Certification Examinations, and she is a guest speaker and clinician on effective interviewing techniques.

Katherine M. Levy

Katherine M. Levy, professor and head of the music education area at the State University of New York at Fredonia, earned Ph.D. and Master's degrees in music education from the University of Iowa, and a B.M.E. from Northwestern University. Her teaching experience includes learners of all ages in instrumental music, general music, and music educator preparation programs in several states in the central and eastern United States. Katherine Levy is Music Director of the New Horizons Band of Western New York, a music learning, concert band, and small ensemble program for older adults, and she has served as a mentor and workshop leader for New Horizons International Music Association. She is an active guest conductor, speaker, and clinician.

INDEX